MW00424978

RHS

Do
BEES NEED
WEEDS?

RHS Do Bees Need Weeds?
Author: Gareth Richards and Holly Farrell
First published in Great Britain in 2020 by Mitchell Beazley, an imprint of
Octopus Publishing Group Ltd, Carmelite House, 50 Victoria Embankment,
London EC4Y 0DZ
www.octopusbooks.co.uk

An Hachette UK Company
www.hachette.co.uk

Published in association with the Royal Horticultural Society
Copyright © Quarto Publishing plc 2020

ISBN: 978 1 78472 7147

A CIP record of this book is available from the British Library
Set in Archer and Open Sans
Printed and bound in China

Mitchell Beazley Publisher: Alison Starling
RHS Publisher: Rae Spencer-Jones
RHS Consultant Editor: Simon Maughan
RHS Head of Editorial: Chris Young

Conceived, designed and produced by
The Bright Press
Part of the Quarto Group
The Old Brewery, 6 Blundell Street, London, N7 9BH, England
Publisher: James Evans
Managing Editor: Jacqui Sayers
Project Editor: Emily Angus
Design and Picture Research: JC Lanaway

The Royal Horticultural Society is the UK's leading gardening charity
dedicated to advancing horticulture and promoting good gardening.
Its charitable work includes providing expert advice and information,
training the next generation of gardeners, creating hands-on opportunities
for children to grow plants and conducting research into plants, pests
and environmental issues affecting gardeners.

For more information visit www.rhs.org.uk or call 0845 130 4646.

Do
BEES NEED
WEEKS?

WEEDS?

A GARDENER'S COLLECTION
of Handy Hints *for*
Greener Gardening

GARETH RICHARDS & HOLLY FARRELL
FOREWORD BY KATE BRADBURY

MITCHELL
BEAZLEY

Contents

4 Wildlife Back-up

5   Re-using and Recycling

Foreword

by Kate Bradbury

Climate change, biodiversity and sustainability are the biggest issues facing our generation, with scientists predicting that we have only a few years to act to limit climate change catastrophe. While we sign petitions and urge governments to act, many of us are turning to our own lifestyles to help fight climate change at home. You might already be flying less and taking public transport more, eating more vegetarian food or even growing your own fruit and vegetables. You might conduct talks and demonstrations at neighbourhood meetings or take part in local events.

But what can we do closer to home? What about that green space outside our back door? Will growing a few vegetables and keeping chickens really make a difference? Is it even possible to garden without plastic and synthetic chemicals? Do you really need to take up paving stones to help the planet?

Gardens in the UK take up more space than all of its nature reserves put together. That's around a fifth of the size of Wales (c. 1600 square miles) of lawns, plants, ponds and trees. Imagine what could we achieve, in the fight against climate change, if we all planted a tree tomorrow, mowed our lawn less often or dug a pond? Or if we all started home composting and stopped using artificial chemicals to grow our plants?

This charming book offers invaluable hints explaining how you can help save the planet by making simple changes to the way you garden. You'll find anything from giving up synthetic chemicals to alternatives to peat, and what to do if you want to stop using plastic pots. The best thing about the book – and the advice it offers – is that you can dip in and out of it. You can choose which changes to make in your garden, discovering what works for you the most.

It's not just the planet that benefits from a more sustainable approach to gardening. By using your garden to create a green corridor, sharing plants with neighbours or planting a green roof, you will also be helping wildlife.

Climate change and biodiversity loss come hand-in-hand and the decline in wildlife is just as worrying as rising sea levels. By actively working to create garden habitats in which wildlife can live, feed and breed, you can help prevent extinctions. Right outside your back door. This book will show you how to do it.

Introduction

DOING SOMETHING POSITIVE for the environment isn't just about donating to rainforest charities or campaigning to end the ivory trade. You can make a difference outside your back door. This book is full of more than 100 innovative, interesting and fun ways we can all 'green up our act'. Gardens have never been more important for wildlife, and this book will help you get the very best out of your plot, for both people and the planet.

Bees, birds and butterflies depend ever more heavily on gardens for their very survival. Nature isn't confined to nature reserves or wild tracts of countryside, anyone with a garden – or any form of outdoor space – can make a meaningful difference. This book is full of fascinating facts, simple tips and low-cost ideas to help you garden in an eco-friendly way.

In the UK alone, private gardens occupy an area one-fifth the size of Wales – so even if you think your garden by itself is too small to make a difference, it's potentially a valuable piece in a very large jigsaw!

The impact of the way we garden is enormous, and the more we can make it sustainable and zero-waste, the better.

This book takes a wide-ranging look at the issues surrounding sustainable gardening. We start by considering the bigger picture – discussing issues such as whether it's ever okay to use chemicals, what 'sustainability' really means and how gardens might evolve in the future with the impact of climate change.

Whether you're faced with an empty plot or a mature garden, you may be wondering where to start?

Every flowering plant in your garden is a positive bonus for our declining but important pollinating insects.

A

QUICK ANSWERS

The 'A' box under each question offers you the 'top line' or most concise answer. Read on for the main text, which offers additional context and plenty of extra detail.

▶ Reusing items such as old tyres can make for inventive, quirky garden features and helps keep waste out of landfill.

Chapter two offers lots of advice on how to arrange your space, what to do with paving and builders' rubble, whether you need to change the layout and replace the soil.

In chapter three we discuss how to make 'growing your own' as green as it can be. Are greenhouses, wormeries and polytunnels worth investing in? Can you get crops from pots? How can you discourage pests without spraying and will you still get a decent harvest?

Many people worry that a wildlife garden has to be untidy and full of nettles. Chapter four is packed with ways to make the very best of your garden for both wildlife and people. It's also full of fascinating information about the species that share our space, to help gardeners understand what makes wildlife tick.

Our final chapter is all about re-using and recycling. As everyone becomes more and more aware of just how damaging our addiction to plastic has become, this is a timely reminder that things weren't always this way. We share lots of cunning ways to reduce, re-use and recycle, plus useful tips on quirky topics from keeping chickens to growing your own dye plants. Going green has never been more necessary – but it's also never been easier or more enjoyable!

◀ However small your garden is, there's a crop you can grow in pots. French bean plants are particularly prolific in their production.

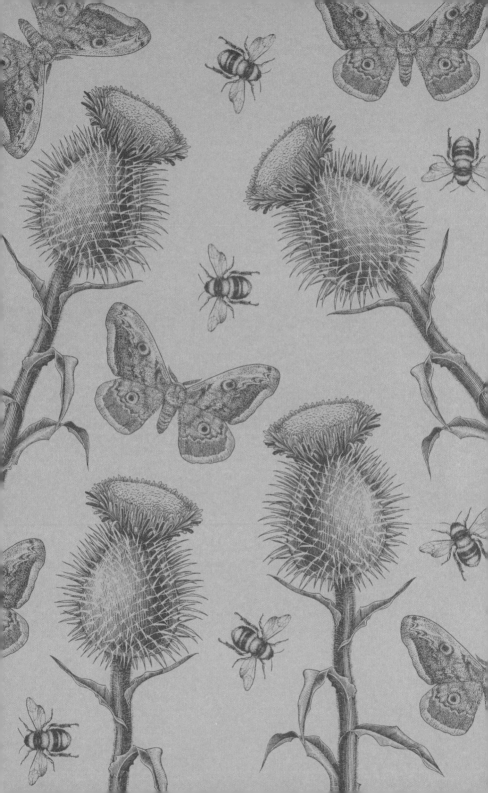

Chapter 1

The Bigger Picture

Are my garden lights harmful?

PLANTS, ANIMALS AND HUMANS all have natural rhythms associated with night and day. For thousands of years, growth and reproductive patterns have relied on knowing when the days were getting longer in spring and shorter in autumn, and natural light dictated whether it was time to sleep or wake. But humans have massively disrupted these rhythms with artificial light.

Unfortunately, yes. Garden lights are harmful to wildlife. Restricting their use and reducing their intensity will help. It's best to get rid of them altogether, but if that is not possible then at least having security lights on sensors will limit their use.

As well as preventing many people from seeing the stars at night, light pollution can have a detrimental effect on wildlife, both on the small scale of a garden and the larger scale of a city. It can take the form of trespass (light from an external source shines in your windows), glare (bright lights can temporarily blind or disorientate) and skyglow, the cumulative effect of light reflecting off airborne dust, creating an orange haze. A large proportion of skyglow is caused by lighting that is unnecessary, including garden lighting.

What can we do to help?

The easiest and quickest action is to stop using lights in the garden (which saves energy too). If they are truly necessary for security or safety (consider if a solar- or hand-crank operated torch will do instead), install sensor-operated lights that turn themselves off after a few minutes, and shield them to directly illuminate only the necessary area. Summer garden parties can be lit by candles, which have a lower intensity and won't be as intrusive or damaging on one-off occasions. Join campaigns against light pollution (such as Nightblight, run by the Campaign to Protect Rural England (CPRE)) and put friendly pressure on your local council and businesses to reduce their use of lights at night, or to at least make them more efficient, such as motion-sensor street lighting, shielded road lights and replacing white glare with lower-wattage, dimmable warm-white bulbs.

Kentish glory moth
Endromis versicolora

Emperor moth
Saturnia pavonia

▶ Garden lights disrupt the feeding
and pollination patterns of moths, and
can potentially lure these nocturnal
fliers into dangerous collisions.

Privet hawk moth
Sphinx ligustri

DISRUPTING NATURAL RHYTHMS

Lighting up the night has a number of negative effects on wildlife:

• The feeding patterns of many animals are disrupted. Birds are awake (and singing) at night when they should be sleeping, and nocturnal foragers no longer have a sense of when it is dark.

• Birds and insects such as moths fly towards the light and collide (fatally) with buildings.

• It is harder to tell when it is spring, so reproduction patterns of many animals and birds are disrupted, especially amphibians.

• Migration patterns of birds are affected.

• Nocturnal pollinators are disrupted, leading to a drop in pollination rates.

• It masks the phases of the moon, which could be affecting coral reproduction in, for example, the Great Barrier Reef.

• When baby sea turtles hatch, they know to head towards the light. The only light used to be the moon reflecting off the sea. Now the brightest lights are often from the towns inshore of the beaches, and many baby turtles head off in the opposite direction to the water, which will prove to be fatal.

• The flowering and growth patterns of plants are affected as cannot detect how long the day or night is, with consequences for crop harvests.

◀ Night-time urban birdsong is a sign of light pollution disrupting natural rhythms.

European wren
Troglodytes troglodytes

Q Are chemicals ever better than the alternative?

IS IT BETTER TO GROW **healthier plants and control plant diseases and pests by using chemical sprays, or are all chemicals ecologically a bad idea?**

Buttercup
Ranunculus

Advantages of chemicals

• Chemical sprays and pellets are quick to respond.
• Fertilisers have an appreciable effect on the growth, flowering and cropping of plants and lawns. Herbicides are an easy way to deal with weeds in borders and paths, taking a lot less effort than removing them by hand.
• Chemicals can bring plant diseases and pest infestations under control, which may mean saving the plant or the crop.

Disadvantages of chemicals

• Most are based on petro-chemicals, come in plastic bottles and take a lot of energy to produce.
• Pesticides are often indiscriminate, killing beneficial insects such as ladybirds, bees and hoverflies as well as the pests, and most insect populations are in trouble.
• Some pests evolve resistance to the pesticides.

A A garden with a healthy natural ecosystem should have little need for chemicals, which are often based on petro-chemicals and indiscriminately harmful to wildlife and the environment, not to mention people. Chemical fertilisers, pesticides and herbicides (weedkillers) are likely to be less available or banned outright in the future anyway.

• Herbicides such as glyphosate are known to persist in crops and ultimately our own bodies – the long-term effects of ingesting these are as yet unknown, but on a global scale (in countries where regulations are more lax) pesticide poisoning in humans is a real problem.
• Fertilisers can get washed into the soil and rivers where they cause algal bloom and disrupt the aquatic ecosystems, harming fish and other wildlife.

◀ Unfortunately, many chemical garden sprays are fatal to all insects, including the beneficial species.

The alternative

Cultivating a healthy garden will go a long way towards limiting or eliminating the need for chemical fertiliser and fungicides. Most problems are usually short-lived and in the wider context of a diverse and environmentally-friendly garden and way of life, increasing one's tolerance for aphids or powdery mildew can be a really helpful step.

How to eliminate the need for chemicals

• Mulch the soil (and top-dress pots) every year with homemade compost, leaf mould or other good-quality organic matter to provide all the nutrient needs of the plants, conserve moisture and suppress weeds.
• Grow plants suited to the garden's soil, sun levels and aspect. Trying to grow the wrong plants will mean they will inevitably be unhealthy.
• Encourage a diverse range of wildlife to the garden, especially beneficial insects such as ladybirds and hoverflies, which will predate on pests.
• Don't over-water, which will either make plants suffocate in waterlogged soil or encourage lush, sappy growth that will attract aphids, slugs and caterpillars.
• Hand-weed, digging out the roots to prevent them coming back. Add ground cover plants to out-compete weeds, or mulch. Removing annual weeds before they have a chance to set seed means fewer chances for weeds next year. Never put the roots of perennial weeds in the compost.
• Dispose of diseased plant material properly by burning to prevent further infection. Keep tools clean and sharp, and prune at the correct time of year, to prevent spreading diseases.

LAST RESORT

Chemical use in gardens should only ever be as a last resort, if it is really necessary and once physical and biological control options have been exhausted. Dispose of old garden chemicals safely and responsibly (contact the council for advice), and always follow the label directions, applying chemicals in a controlled and safe manner that limits their impact to the target plant. Unofficial plant treatments, such as dilute washing-up liquid and garlic-based sprays, should also only be a last resort and the more natural the origin the better: these options cannot be recommended by bodies such as the RHS but they are not illegal for the home grower.

Q Is it ever okay to have a bonfire?

I HAVE A LOT OF TREES AND SHRUBS in my garden,
which creates a lot of woody waste and leaves in the autumn.
I usually burn all of this, but is it bad for global warming?

A Bonfires are occasionally
necessary to dispose of
diseased plant material, but
composting waste is a far better
option for the environment.

Why are bonfires bad for the world?

Bonfires release heat and carbon into
the atmosphere as they burn, and
while the contribution of your home
bonfire to overall global warming may
be tiny, every little helps. The smoke
also adds to air pollution. Wildlife such
as insects and hedgehogs that may be
nesting in the pile will not be able to
escape the flames.

▼ Collecting fallen autumn leaves
into sacks to make leaf mould is a
greener alternative to a bonfire.

When is a bonfire needed?

The only time gardeners need to have a
bonfire is in the case of diseased plant
material or invasive perennial weeds:
composting this could perpetuate
the disease or the weed, whether in
a home heap or taken to a municipal
one. Burning is the best way to
remove the diseased material or weed
permanently, but burn only this rather
than piling on lots of healthy material.

Burning potential

Instead, use fallen leaves to make
compost or leaf mould, which is a
fantastic mulch for any soil and very
easy to make. Simply collect up the
leaves, spray with water if they are dry,
and leave to rot. They can be put into
old compost sacks (punch a few holes
in the sides for air circulation),
or make cages out of wooden stakes
and chicken wire. Leave until rotted
and crumbly.

Woody plant waste can be made
into a dead hedge or log pile (see
p. 190), chopped up and added to
the compost heap, or taken to the
local recycling centre's green waste
collection.

Should I stop using plastic pots?

I KNOW PLASTIC CREATES a lot of problems for the environment, so I don't want to use it in my garden anymore. I use plastic pots a lot – should I get rid of them all?

Getting rid of perfectly usable pots, whatever they are made of, makes no environmental sense. A better option is to use everything, plastic pots included, until it is at the end of its life, and then replace it with a non-plastic, environmentally-friendly alternative.

Re-using cardboard – such as egg cartons – is a great alternative to plastic trays for raising seedlings.

Until recently, the horticultural industry used black plastic pots to grow and sell almost every plant. Pressure from consumers has led to a rethink, and recyclable or biodegradable alternatives are now being trialled and used by many firms. However, many gardeners still have a stock of black plastic pots in the shed or greenhouse, and throwing these away is not the answer.

Reduce

When buying new plants, seek out companies that supply plants in biodegradable or recyclable packaging rather than plastic of any sort, or grow from seed yourself.

Re-use

If a pot is not cracked or broken, keep re-using it until it perishes, either to grow on seedlings and cuttings, or to house plants you are giving away. If you can't re-use the pots, find out if a local gardening charity, school garden or other community scheme might want them. Getting the maximum benefit out of it at least lowers its overall impact on the environment.

Recycle

Only once a plastic pot has reached the end of its useful life should it be disposed of. In response to demand, many garden centre chains are offering recycling bins for black plastic pots (which cannot be recycled by the local council).

Can I convert my neighbours to greener habits?

I AM DOING WHAT I CAN to make my garden and lifestyle more environmentally friendly, but my neighbours don't seem to care. How can I persuade them to adopt greener ways of gardening?

Everybody has the capacity to change, they just need the right motivation and support. Converting neighbours and friends to greener habits might take a while, but even the most hardened climate-sceptic will probably want to help protect hedgehogs.

if everyone thinks that their own personal actions make no difference, no one will act, so encourage them with stories of small changes adding up to big transformations in the wider community. It's also important not to use every conversation as a chance to convert them – a softly, softly approach over a long time is more likely to yield results than wielding a big proverbial environmental stick every time you see them.

Tone

It's important not to preach or be patronising. Your neighbours may have very good reasons for doing what they do (or don't do) in the garden, or they may be doing it out of ignorance or habit, but until you empathise with their point of view, they are unlikely to listen to yours. It's hard to ignore climate advice these days, so if a neighbour has distinctly un-green garden habits it is possible they either don't understand the problem or don't see how they can make a difference. They may think they don't have time to garden. But

Lead by example

Getting to know your neighbour over the garden fence has a wealth of opportunities to show what you are doing successfully in your garden, such as growing without chemicals or plastic, growing fruit and veg or making provision for

▶ Encourage your neighbours into greener habits by sharing stories of garden wildlife and hampers of home-grown produce.

Apple tree
Malus domestica

wildlife, and might encourage them to try it themselves. If they are complaining about a problem in their garden, suggest green ways to deal with it and even offer to help.

Get your facts straight

Climate sceptics are best managed using facts rather than impassioned rhetoric. If your neighbours tell you they don't believe in climate change, inform them of a few simple facts, such as the last five years have been the hottest on record, and that carbon dioxide levels are higher now than in any other time in human history. If they quote a climate-sceptic scientist, you could point out that 99 percent of the scientific community believe that global warming is caused by human activity.

Make it personal

Humans are ultimately selfish, and will respond better to threats or benefits to their own existence than to that of the wider world. Point out that flooding is less likely in the area if rain run-off is reduced by converting paved driveways to gardens. If they complain about littering, use it to start a conversation about single-use items and non-biodegradable waste. Food is expensive? Grow your own. Relate wider issues to personal experience – for example, a fall in biodiversity is evidenced by fewer species of butterflies and birds visiting our gardens.

FOCUS ON THE BENEFITS OF BEING GREEN

Making the community greener by planting trees and wildflowers, or starting up community projects, will encourage people to join in (so you can then demonstrate greener methods). Appeal to the cute factor (hedgehogs are a real crowd-pleaser) when encouraging changes in garden habits to help wildlife. Show 'old-school' gardeners that by underplanting their prize roses with weed-suppressing lambs ear (*Stachys byzantina*) or periwinkle (*Vinca* spp.) they can eliminate the cost of herbicide sprays, and help the bees that pollinate their fruit cage. Convert harassed families or young professionals to taking care of their patch by showing what good stress-relief gardening can be.

Q Can my garden be a green corridor?

I KNOW WILDLIFE CAN SOMETIMES have a hard time moving around cities and towns, and finding food. What can I do to help connect my garden to the bigger picture of supporting wildlife in my area?

What is a green corridor?

A green, or wildlife, corridor is a series of linked green spaces – gardens, parks and hedgerows – that interconnect the spaces with each other and the wider surrounding countryside and enable wildlife to circumvent buildings and roads. They help to provide habitat links between nesting and foraging sites for wildlife, and have tree and shrub cover for safe movement and a variation in planted species to offer diverse feeding opportunities for different creatures.

A Simply growing a variety of plants in your garden will make it an attractive pit stop. To make it part of something bigger, surround it with as much greenery as possible, working with neighbours, the council and local wildlife charities. Ensure that fences and walls can be got through or around by creatures that can't fly.

How to connect your garden to the wider green surroundings

Join the local community group – or start one – and initiate more green spaces in the neighbourhood such as wildflower verges and street trees will expand the corridor outwards. Use a map to work out the best way to interconnect the local green spaces. Encourage the council to add more municipal planting, such as green

walls, (see p. 28) or change the way they manage existing spaces to better support wildlife. Local businesses might be interested in sponsoring green spaces or planters in front of their shops and offices.

Get in touch and work with the local wildlife trust and other gardening and wildlife charities – they may also have specific local issues that need help, such as toad crossings.

Making a beeline

Providing a nectar-rich garden will help bees, butterflies and other insects move around in towns and cities, and be a pit stop when they are tired and hungry. Use the RHS Plants for Pollinators lists (and look out for the bee logo on plant labels) to help choose new flowering plants, shrubs and trees for the garden that will specifically help feed pollinating insects.

The insect charity Buglife also has a campaign to help bees, butterflies and other insects, creating a network of 'B-lines', flower-rich interconnected pathways to provide a network of habitats and feeding grounds for the UK's insects across the countryside, towns and cities. Find out more on their website: buglife.org.uk

Hedgehog highways

Hedgehogs can roam up to 1 mile (2km) in a single night looking for food, 1½ miles (3km) in the breeding season, so ensuring they can move between gardens and other green spaces is crucial for their wellbeing. Make sure there are suitably sized holes in the walls and fences around your property – 13cm^2 (5 in^2) is big enough, and too small for most pets. Encourage your neighbours to do the same. It's also important to raise awareness of hedgehog activity amongst local residents and drivers on the road so that everyone drives mindfully of hedgehogs.

▶ Even small gardens are valuable pit stops for wildlife to feed and rest on their wider journeys around the neighbourhood.

What should I do with invasive green waste?

I KNOW I SHOULD COMPOST as much as possible from my garden, but what should I do about invasive weeds? Can I put them on the compost or do I need to do something different with them?

What is an invasive plant?

Although some plants are terrible weeds if allowed to take over a garden, such as ground elder or bindweed, these are not officially classed as invasive. It is still not a good idea to put them in the compost however, as they can come back and re-infest the soil from even small sections of root. Burn the waste instead.

Invasive plants have been designated by the government as a threat to the native ecosystem (they are usually non-native species), and all efforts are made to stop them spreading and reduce their numbers. Examples include Japanese knotweed, giant hogweed and Himalayan balsam, but a full list can be found on the Environment Agency website. Note that this list includes a number of aquatic plants as well.

How do I get rid of it?

Once as much of the plant has been dug up as possible (and this is a process that may need to be repeated many times over several years to slowly weaken and eventually kill

Persistent and invasive weeds are best burnt or disposed of professionally; plants listed as invasive have legislation attached to their control and disposal, so check with the local council.

the plant), some species, including invasive aquatic plants, can be burnt. It is also possible to apply a sustained programme of herbicide spraying, but again this must be repeated regularly over many years, and chemical herbicides are increasingly unavailable for domestic gardeners.

Contact your local council to get details of suitable contractors who can undertake a control (spraying) or disposal programme: Japanese knotweed, Himalayan balsam and giant hogweed all need to be disposed of using a registered waste carrier, which will usually incur a cost.

Are seed- and plant-swaps always a good idea?

LOCAL COMMUNITIES and gardening clubs often host seed and plant swaps in spring, sometimes in conjunction with potato days (to buy seed potatoes). This is more organised than swapping plants and cuttings with a friend, but is one better than the other?

Since gardeners first started gardening, they have swapped seeds and exchanged plant material, and it is a great way to expand your garden and your knowledge for free, provided you are careful not to spread pests and diseases.

A seed swap isn't just a chance to pick up a packet of some seeds of a plant you'd really like to have in the garden, it's also an opportunity to meet new people with similar interests and quiz knowledgeable gardeners. It's a chance to get out, to get enthused about the garden again when spring is just around the corner. It's also an opportunity to pass on spare packets of seeds (perhaps you over-ordered) and have a go at sowing something you've never grown before.

Potential problems

Although a seed swap might have been organised by a local charity or club, there is often no control over the quality of the material being exchanged, so it's usually a case of buyer (or swapper) beware when taking home plants or seeds. Quarantining new plants is always a good idea, in case of diseases, and giving them a thorough check over for pests and general health before taking them. Seeds could no longer be viable, or collected/stored improperly, meaning they don't germinate, or don't match the name on the packet.

Index Seminum

The *Index Seminum*, a seed-exchange scheme between many botanic and physic gardens, was started between the Chelsea Physic Garden and Leiden University Botanic Garden in the seventeenth century and continues to this day. RHS members can order seed collected in the RHS gardens (for a nominal charge to cover processing and postage costs). Sharing seed in this way helps to preserve endangered species and increase global biodiversity.

What do people mean when they call plants native?

IS A NATIVE PLANT simply one that grows wild in the countryside, or are there more precise criteria? Are natives better for wildlife and the environment than exotic plants from far-off lands?

In Britain, the established definition of native is that the plant has grown there since the end of the last Ice Age. While this does give some indication that a plant may be useful to wildlife, it's not an excuse to discount non-natives as they can be ecologically very valuable too, particularly in the future as the climate changes.

Sycamore
Acer pseudoplatanus

It's a somewhat arbitrary definition, but traditionally, in Britain at least, a plant is considered native if it arrived before the landmass became an island, approximately 8,000 years ago. Only about 1,500 plants made it in the short time between the last Ice Age and the climate warming up enough for life to flourish before sea levels rose and cut Britain off.

The plants and animals of Britain hadn't finished adapting to the new post-glacial age by the time this 'native' cut-off point occured. Britain's native flora is represented by the quickest, most rampaging species that arrived after the ice retreated; France, its nearest neighbour, has twice the land area but more than three times the native plant species.

Luckily, some might say, humans have helped redress the balance and our total number of wild plants is almost doubled by the presence of 1,400 feral non-natives. Most of these are well-behaved and some are much loved: corncockles, conker trees and common poppies to name but a few. Only a small number (such as Japanese knotweed) are problem invaders, and they tend to establish mostly on brownfield sites. Most of our worst and most widespread weeds are native: bracken ('if bracken wasn't native it would be declared a national emergency' according to ecologist Ken Thompson), brambles, thistles, nettles...

What about wildlife?

The RHS Plants for Bugs study was a four-year experiment to find out whether garden insects preferred native plants. To broadly summarise, the results indicate that the best way to have a wildlife-friendly garden is to include lots of native plants, but to add some non-natives too. To quote the authors: 'Any planting is better than none, and diversity of plant origin in a garden is a strength, not a weakness.'

THE PROBLEM WITH OUR DEFINITION OF 'NATIVE'

There are a few problems with this definition. The main one is that it is completely arbitrary, and makes no allowance for the fact that nature isn't static and constant: it's dynamic, living, breathing and ever-changing. What was native 10,000 years ago might not really be native now, as our environment and climate have changed considerably. Back in 1992, scientists calculated that the rate that some plant species could shift their ranges was ten times too slow to keep up with the rate of climate change.

Common poppy
Papaver rhoeas

Thistle
Cirsium vulgare

Bluebell
Hyacinthoides non-scripta

Cornflower
Centaurea cyanus

How will gardening change in the next 20 years?

How will the changing climate affect our gardens in the future? What other trends are there that will have an impact on gardening?

Gardens, and the plants within them, can be a source of constancy in a whirlwind world, but they can also help us face the challenges of the future. Gardens are likely to be more personal spaces, and havens for both us and wildlife, planted to adapt to more extreme climate events.

planting for the most likely events in your area. Campaigns to plant more trees and front gardens will continue, in order to help reduce urban water run-off. More green walls and roofs will be incorporated into buildings to help with heat insulation and air pollution.

Milder winters will extend the growing season, but the traditional flowering times of many plants will

Wellbeing

As more people realise the benefits of getting outside, and the therapeutic effect gardening can have on the body and mind, gardens will be personal retreats from the world, and there will be more community gardens and municipal green spaces as social prescribing grows.

Climate

As climate change brings more extreme weather and weather events, such as drought, high temperatures, strong winds and flooding, gardens will need to adapt with suitable

Living wall

Potato

be affected. Planting a wide range of flowering plants will ensure plenty of food throughout the season for pollinators and other insects.

Forest gardening – a style of growing that is already proven to withstand extreme weather events very well – is likely to become more prevalent even in small back gardens.

Grow your own

Fruit and vegetable growing will continue to be popular – and perhaps councils will allocate fresh land for allotments as waiting lists continue to grow – concern over the negative effects on wildlife of large-scale mono-culture increases, and people become more aware of the benefits of organic food. We are beginning to understand how reliant we are on imported food and the 'just in time' policies of supermarkets, some will grow their own to be more self-sufficient. Herb growing could also see a renewed surge in interest, as science starts to return to using plant-based medicines, and people turn to alternative health.

Wildlife gardening

Petro-chemical-derived pesticides, herbicides and fungicides will continue to be banned for domestic use, meaning gardeners have to adapt to more natural methods of gardening. This will largely be driven by concern for insect populations and other wildlife, which will also result in more efforts being made to plant for pollinators, and provide wildlife habitats in domestic gardens. The average 'lawn and borders' garden will have more biodiversity. Wildlife feeding, breeding and hibernation patterns will be affected by milder winters.

Imported and exotic pests and diseases

New plant diseases and pest threats could increase if a demand for cheap garden plants continues to rise, as large-scale growers import from abroad. Changing weather conditions will mean changes in insects and other wildlife as populations move to seek the climate they prefer – this could mean more exotic species extending their range.

Houseplants and potted plants

Growing plants in rented accommodation, such as balcony gardens and indoor displays, will continue to grow in popularity, if house prices continue to be unattainable for the younger generation.

Q Is sustainability the same everywhere?

LOTS OF COMPANIES talk about their sustainable credentials, and I see the words 'sustainable source' on packaging. What does it mean, and is it the same the world over?

A In environmental terms sustainability means a product or service that doesn't deplete natural resources. In the garden, that translates as being self-sufficient in things like compost and water use. There may be companies that apply the word 'sustainable' to their products erroneously in order to increase sales, so do your homework before making a purchase.

Sustainability is the ability to maintain a certain level or rate of growth, and in an environmental context that usually means maintaining the status quo with regard to the depletion of natural resources. For example, a paper company would be able to call itself sustainable if it planted trees to replace all those it cut down to make paper products (although this doesn't take into account the fact that a forest of sapling trees (especially if a monoculture forest) cannot provide the same wildlife habitat, carbon and water storage, or soil erosion benefits that a forest of mature trees can).

To be truly sure a company or product is sustainable it is best to do some background research before making a purchase. Only by knowing all the facts can we, as consumers, make a conscious choice about which companies to support.

In the garden, sustainability is achieved by re-using and recycling as much as possible – making your own compost and leaf mould for example, and choosing the right plants for the situation to avoid the need to water and feed as much as possible, and install a water butt and make comfrey tea for when you do need to water and feed the plants. Avoid using imported products and those that deplete natural resources (such as peat-based potting compost), and don't use chemical fertilisers, pesticides or herbicides.

My garden is in a sea of concrete, how can it help?

I HAVE A SMALL FRONT GARDEN that I have filled with plants, but all around me are blocks of flats and offices that have no greenery at all. Is my garden actually going to make any difference to wildlife populations, reducing urban heat and rain run-off, or is my plot insignificant?

Although it may seem your garden is a solitary green drop in a sea of concrete, there may be other gardens closer than you think. There are an estimated 24 million domestic gardens in the UK, which make up an interconnected mosaic of plants, food and habitats for wildlife, and contribute to carbon storage, reducing air and noise pollution and rain run-off. They also make our towns and cities nicer places to live. By using your garden to its full potential (for example, growing plants up the walls) and adding in bird feeders and bug hotels, you can make it a haven for you and the local wildlife.

▶ Using the vertical space in your garden for climbing plants can provide more food and nesting sites for wildlife.

If you have local businesses nearby, why not volunteer to maintain some borders or planters around their frontage? You get to have a little more garden to play with and increase the local garden space, and they only have to pay out a little money for plants and supplies in return for adding beauty and interest to their building (which will no doubt be appreciated by their staff and clients).

Set a green example

Seeing your garden, and what a difference it can make to personal wellbeing and also potential house prices, might encourage your neighbours to start gardening too. Help them out if they are beginners – give them seeds and plants, and advice if they ask for it – and hopefully the greenery will start to spread.

Don't lose faith! Every tiny patch of green garden does help the environment and wildlife, and seeing how lovely your garden is will hopefully inspire others to get gardening too.

Is there any proof that gardening is good for your health?

LOTS OF PEOPLE SAY that gardening is good for your physical and mental health, but isn't this just anecdotal evidence? Have there been any scientific studies?

Gardening for the body...

• Gardening is good exercise. It gets the body moving in a gentle way and lifting and bending builds muscle strength. Half an hour of gardening uses an equivalent number of calories to half an hour of playing badminton. Nature is distracting for the brain, so we will spend longer exercising outside than we would inside, reducing our stress levels at the same time.

• Contact with the soil, and the beneficial microbes that live in it, improves the health of our gut microbiome, which in turn boosts our immunity levels. The earlier we are exposed to the soil the better, so it's a great idea to garden with children.

• Growing our own (organic) fruit and vegetables provides us with a variety of nourishing foods, consumed straight from the garden these will have higher levels of vitamins than those that have been on the shop shelf for a while.

• Access to herbs can support our overall health, such as fresh mint tea for aiding digestion, or a rosemary hair rinse for a healthy scalp.

Yes, plenty of studies have shown that gardening is an excellent pastime for everybody, with significant benefits to physical strength and fitness as well as contributing in many ways to our mental wellbeing.

• Houseplants act as air filters, removing and storing from the air harmful particles and toxins from pollution, paint and electrical devices.

▼ Herbs are nutritious and flavourful but also provide a fragrant trigger to make being in the garden more mindful.

... and for the mind

• The garden can be a haven or retreat, a distraction from a busy or stressful life. Conversely, it can be a way to get out and meet people, combating the feelings of loneliness and isolation that can lead to depression and physical symptoms. A study in 2016 showed that allotment holders and gardeners benefited from the chance to make friends and integrate into the community. The work of horticultural therapists has helped thousands of people cope with and recover from (mental) illness and injury.

• Creating a garden has been shown to help us feel more grounded and at home, especially in a new area.

• Simply being in nature – any green space – has been proven to increase feelings of self-worth and improve mood, including for children.

• Gardening is a mindful activity, encouraging focus on the task at hand not the thoughts swirling around our brains. There is plenty of research showing that even short bursts of mindfulness every day are beneficial for our mental health, lowering stress and improving focus.

• A garden is full of therapeutic scents, sights and sounds. Studies have shown how the scent of rosemary increases our capacity to remember things – especially future tasks, such as remembering to pick up a prescription. Water is either calming or exciting to

 Birdsong has been shown to be calming to the mind, and the birds' antics in the garden are endlessly diverting.

Song thrush
Turdus pilaris

HELPING THE PLANET

In the wider environment, plants help to reduce air pollution and increase urban carbon storage, helping the planet overall. A 2018 study found that planting a hedge instead of a wall or fence in the front garden can also significantly reduce the volume of black carbon coming from the road towards the house (by up to 63 per cent) – especially at the breathing height of children.

our minds, depending on if it is moving or not, and different colours can have different effects on the brain (e.g. hot colours excite, greens are soothing, etc.). Listening to bird song has been shown to reduce stress levels.

If you don't have a garden, what's the best way to help?

I REALLY WANT TO INCREASE the amount of biodiverse greenery there is in the world, and I'd love to brush up my horticultural skills, but I don't have any space in which to grow plants outside. How can I garden without a garden?

There are lots of opportunities to do some gardening, from sharing a garden with a neighbour to volunteering with the RHS. All of the options contribute to making the planet a greener, more pleasant place to live and provide a good chance to learn useful skills and meet new people.

Community gardening

Working with other local people to beautify and green the neighbourhood is not only a chance to do some gardening in a place where you will see it regularly, it also has proven effects on boosting local self-esteem, neighbourhood pride and reducing anti-social behaviour. Community gardeners might have a dedicated space that they maintain – an actual garden – or they might collectively manage a host of smaller spaces such as verges, planters and street trees. Seek out groups in local newsletters, posters in local shops, online or by simply approaching them when they are working to ask if you can join in – the answer will invariably be yes!

Volunteering

Most large public gardens have volunteers working for them as well as paid staff, but there are also lots of smaller, local charities that rely on the help of volunteers to maintain and grow their gardens. Often you will be working alongside a trained horticulturalist, so it's a great way to learn more about gardening, and it's also a chance to meet new people and contribute to the upkeep and work of the garden or charity.

The RHS in the UK, for example, runs a variety of umbrella campaigns aimed at getting communities gardening together.

Garden sharing

Allotment waiting lists are often very long and it can take years to get your own plot. Instead, ask the site administrator if anyone who already has a plot would consider sharing it. This can be a great way to get the chance to do some gardening, get a little produce and make new friends. It might be that there is someone on the site who doesn't want to give up their plot but can no longer maintain it to a good standard – joining forces is a win-win for everybody.

Similarly, what about assisting a friend in their garden? They may welcome the chance to have someone help with the weeding, and it could be a chance to develop the garden further once there are two of you working in it. Plus it's an opportunity to chat and develop a friendship. Alternatively, a friend or neighbour may have a garden that they are not interested in at all, or are no longer able to maintain. Why not offer to look after it for them? They get a more beautiful garden to enjoy with none of the work, and you get the chance to garden and plant a space with a little more autonomy.

▼ Volunteering in a local garden is a great way to learn about horticulture and make new friends.

Do invasive plants invariably reduce biodiversity?

I THOUGHT WE SHOULD be growing a wide range of plants in our gardens, not just native species – are all exotic species invasive and a bad idea?

An invasive species is one that reproduces and grows quickly, spreads aggressively, and unbalances or causes harm to the existing ecosystem. Most plants that are now considered invasive and are subject to government control were introduced as ornamental species, such as Japanese knotweed. Invasive species can also be native species, relatively new introductions, or exotic species that have been here for a long time; all pose a continuous threat to the biodiversity of a country's flora and fauna.

The vast majority of non-native species contribute enormously to biodiversity, and it is only a small number of exotic and native species that are considered invasive.

Invasive species

These species threaten biodiversity in several ways:
1. They outcompete native species by being more vigorous, squeezing out the other plants from the soil or blocking out their light. Invasive species usually have an extremely efficient means of propagating

Exotic species – non-native plants – are on the whole a good idea. A small group of exotic and native species are classed as invasive due to their habit of spreading widely and vigorously; these are extremely detrimental to biodiversity.

themselves, either by running roots or spreading seed (e.g. Himalayan balsam).
2. They import or are hosts for diseases that they themselves do not suffer from but which can have a detrimental effect on other plants.
3. Invasive species spread widely because they can easily adapt to different growing situations and therefore threaten a broad range of habitats.
4. An invasive plant can upset the natural balance of an area sometimes to the extent that eventually they are the only species growing there. Wherever possible, invasive species should be controlled rigorously, in consultation with a specialist.

How long does it take to get a garden in balance 'naturally'?

I'VE STOPPED USING all chemical pesticides, fungicides and fertilisers in my garden and switched to gardening organically, but there are now a lot of aphids. How long will it be before I have an ecosystem that can look after itself?

Rose leaf black spot

Every garden is different, so it's difficult to put a number on how long it will take, but like any aspect of gardening, converting to organic methods requires patience. Although it is easy to give up chemicals overnight, the garden will take time to adjust to the new paradigm.

In the short term, depending on what time of year you make the change, organic gardening can mean a loss of quality and quantity as the pests multiply freely and the plants are less productive without their fertiliser crutch. Balance in the garden is always precarious, and environmental factors out of your control can often cause setbacks, e.g. some years are worse than others for blackfly. But don't lose heart. Often these imbalances sort themselves out in time.

It also takes time to build up the healthy, rich soil that will be the backbone of your organic garden. The Soil Association requires that land be managed organically for two years before it will consider certifying it as organic, indicating the length of time that non-organic treatments take to break down and be washed out of the soil. Natural fertility builds up over years of adding good quality compost and organic matter such as leaf mould to the surface. By rotating vegetable crops for a few years, and burning diseased material (e.g. fallen rose leaves with black spot), the cycles of pest and/or disease infection from the soil will be broken.

In an organic garden, pests can be kept in check using natural controls such as beneficial insects. Initially, these will be at insufficient levels because previously they either didn't have enough pests to eat, or they themselves were being wiped out with the chemical sprays. Make new provisions for encouraging beneficial wildlife into the garden and it will help speed up the rebalancing of pest populations.

Q Why are there lots of some insects and none of others?

INSECTS MAKE UP around two-thirds of all life on earth, and yet their numbers are declining massively, a change scientists are calling a collapse, warning that it will have dire consequences for the rest of the world's living species, including us. Among the British insects in serious decline are moths, butterflies, bees and beetles, yet our gardens are full of aphids and ants in the summertime, so why are some insect populations falling when others seem to be thriving?

A In fact, we don't know if some insect species are declining at faster rates than others because there isn't sufficient data to compare them; or it may be that some insects are particularly badly affected by loss of habitat and pesticide sprays. Either way, it's crucial to do whatever we can to protect them.

While the insect population is plummeting in general, at a rate of extinction eight times faster than mammals, some species seem to be worse affected. For example, on farmed land, the number of butterflies and moths fell by 58 per cent between 2000 and 2009, compared with a rate of 2.5 per cent for insects overall.

Lies, damned lies and statistics

It may be that insect species are falling at comparable rates across the board, but because some species are studied more than others – and some countries are doing more research – it skews the data. If no one has information on the number of, for example, blackfly, their numbers could be falling but we just don't know about it. Those species that are studied (and are more photogenic and appealing) make the headlines.

▲▶ Why not monitor insect levels in your own garden as a citizen scientist for a picture of local biodiversity?

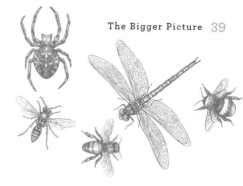

INVASIVE SPECIES

Sometimes decline in one species can be linked to another factor: being outcompeted by an invasive species. The arrival in the country of harlequin ladybirds (1) has left Britain's native ladybirds (2) struggling to find food, because the harlequins are far more voracious eaters of aphids. Furthermore, the harlequins will also eat the eggs and larvae of the native ladybirds, further reducing their numbers.

disappears, such as hedgerows or meadows, those insects will naturally suffer disproportionately. European grassland butterflies are known to have been badly affected in this way, although when studies were made of the whole of the indigenous insect populations it was revealed that their decline was far from unique.

Farming and horticultural practices that use pesticide sprays wipe out insects on the land indiscriminately – intensive monoculture and the pesticide sprays it requires is one of the main drivers behind insect population losses. For example, neonicotinoid pesticide sprays have been highlighted by environmental campaigners as especially harmful for their negative effects on bees, leading to some bans. However, other sprays still in use not only kill insects on the crops but also sterilise the soil, killing insects and larvae there, too.

The other factor to consider is that at the base of the food pyramid there will always be greater numbers than the higher tiers – so there will always be more aphids than the hoverflies that predate upon them.

Habitat loss

A major factor in insect decline is habitat loss: there simply aren't as many plants and green areas for them to live in as there used to be, and there are fewer plants for them to feed on. Where there are insects that live only in a particular habitat that then

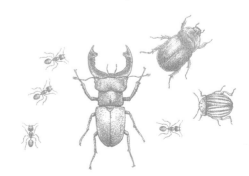

Will global warming bring different species to the garden?

A WARMER CLIMATE **means we can grow a wider range of plants – but is this an opportunity or a threat to our gardens? What kinds of plants are we likely to see in the garden in the future, and which will disappear?**

Cyclamen
Cyclamen hederifolium

The major 2017 RHS report *Gardening in a Changing Climate* includes some details on the likely changes of plant species in UK gardens in the future. It is important to note that non-native plants have been growing in the UK for hundreds of years, and of the 14,000 or so plant species known in the UK, only around 10 per cent are truly native to the British Isles. The rest are alien, but not necessarily invasive. The report records changes already seen by UK gardeners and predicts how this is likely to continue. There will be a general shift towards the poles of species in response to a warming climate, and overall milder weather will mean gardeners can plant more exotics like tree ferns and bananas, and grow fruit and vegetables that need long, hot summers like sweet potatoes (while many traditional vegetables will produce lower yields). However, gardeners should be wary of extreme weather events such as very cold snaps that could kill off exotic species.

It is very difficult to predict exactly how flora and fauna will react to the changing climate, but two major studies in the UK have both predicted that there will be a northwards shift of plant species, making it difficult to grow some plants whilst enabling others to flourish. We need to take extra care to ensure alien species do not become invasive.

More southerly species will see their range expand and, where the existing ecosystem is weakened due to climate change, some exotic plants can take advantage and outcompete them. This poses the risk that currently non-threatening non-natives, such

CHANGES IN PESTS AND DISEASES

It is not just the plant species that will change in our gardens, the pests and diseases will be different too. The warmer climate will favour exotic pests and diseases, making them more prevalent, because not only will they be able to overwinter where they previously couldn't, but the range of plant species they favour will also expand. Glasshouse thrips – which previously could only survive on indoor plants – are now found outdoors in the UK. Mildews, which prefer hot and humid conditions, are likely to occur more often and spread faster through infected plants.

UK, is now self-seeding into parks and woodlands around the southern counties, indicating it is thriving.

The *National Plant Monitoring Scheme*, through which citizen scientists collect data that is collated and analysed by botanists, released the findings from its first five-year study in 2020. The wildflowers of various different habitats were surveyed, and they found that wildflowers are moving north because they can't survive droughts in the south. For example, certain wild orchid species have now been seen in the north of the UK for the first time. Other plants such as wild thyme, that can survive drought, are increasing in incidence. The survey also noted that these changes are all happening faster than predicted.

as the holm oak (*Quercus ilex*), will become invasive. *Gunnera tinctora* – an ornamental garden escapee – has already been declared invasive in Ireland. Other examples include cyclamen, which are likely to face extinction as they cannot move north fast enough to get to the cooler weather they need. On the other hand, the palm tree *Trachycarpus fortunei*, once an exotic specimen seen only in the mildest gardens around the

Chinese windmill palm
Trachycarpus fortunei

Can a big garden attract more species than a small one?

I ONLY HAVE A SMALL BACK GARDEN, but I want to make it as wildlife-friendly as possible. How likely is it that I am going to be able to support a really interesting range of wild species?

Climbing honeysuckle
Lonicera

Where a small garden suffers by comparison to a larger wildlife garden, is its reduced ability to offer the space for varied shelter options (i.e. homes) and sufficient food sources to the bigger wildlife species such as mammals, reptiles, amphibians and some bird species. Smaller gardens are also, by their nature, likely to be in built-up areas where land comes at a premium, and there are fewer surrounding gardens with which to share wildlife.

However, the kind of habitats and food sources on offer matters more than size. A small garden with well-stocked borders of floriferous and berry-laden shrubs and trees, perennials with a long season of flowers and seed heads left standing in the autumn, a pond, a wildflower lawn, a log pile and an untidy nettle patch are all going to be home to a wider range and greater number of wildlife species than a large garden with a bowling-green lawn and bedding plants in narrow borders. Maximise the quantity and variety of potential shelter options and food within the garden by, for example, having a small pond, bird feeder and bug hotels, and using the vertical space as well as the horizontal by cladding the walls and fences with climbing plants.

Don't forget that your garden is not an island – it is part of a network of millions of gardens, other green spaces and the countryside. If a small garden is connected to these on the ground, as well as aerially, it still offers the chance for wildlife to visit.

The range of wildlife that a small garden can attract can be surprising. It might not be able to get the most photogenic or appealing species, but it is definitely possible to create a biodiverse habitat that supports a vast number of insects and birds, and maybe even some amphibians, reptiles and mammals.

Is it more important to provide food than shelter?

WHAT SHOULD I CONCENTRATE on providing in my wildlife garden: feeding sites and food plants for different species, or nesting boxes and other places for them to live?

Ideally, a garden would offer both food and shelter for a range of species, but it is often not possible to do this because of size restrictions. Whatever you can provide in your garden will go a long way towards helping wildlife thrive there.

To a certain extent, the balance between providing food or shelter for wildlife is your choice: do you want wildlife to visit the garden, or to live there permanently? Only by providing suitable habitats will garden visitors be tempted to become residents. It may be that you have pets that would make adding a hedgehog house unsuitable, or you would be concerned for the fate of fledgling birds with the neighbouring traffic, so it would be better to only provide food. On the other hand, if there is a localised need to support a particular species (ask your local wildlife trust), you may want to join in the effort by providing shelter in your garden.

Offer whatever you can in your space, providing as many different habitats and food sources as possible for a variety of species (but remember that wildlife will not necessarily want to live cheek-by-jowl). Start by making it suitable for the bottom of the food chain: insects will then encourage the next tier of wildlife.

Observing what comes to take advantage of your new habitats can also inform future choices; if you get a lot of avian visitors but no frogs in the pond, you could choose to concentrate on homes for birds and insects rather than amphibians. However, be patient: wildlife takes time to spread and move into new spaces, and having a welcoming garden full of food and shelter means they are more likely to make it home.

▼ Birds also benefit from extra food during their nesting and breeding season.

Blackbird nest

Q What do bats need?

I'D LIKE TO HELP nocturnal visitors to my garden, not just daytime ones. Are bats in decline? What can I do to help them?

Common pipistrelle
Pipistrellus pipistrellus

A Bats are amazing creatures with an undeserved reputation for being creepy or spooky, no doubt due to their association with vampires and derelict houses. Their presence indicates a healthy and diverse ecosystem, so they are the crowning glory of a wildlife garden. A few simple additions to your garden can help to support and encourage bats to visit.

Bats are important predators of insects and also the only pollinators of some desert plants. Worldwide, they can help re-forest cleared areas by dispersing the seeds of the fruit they eat. In the UK, bats occupy a variety of habitats, including urban areas as well as woodlands, wetlands and farmland. They are sensitive to changes in these habitats, so monitoring the bat populations can give an early warning sign of a fall in biodiversity or that habitat losses are going too far.

Bats are the only true flying mammal in the world. An evolutionary oddity that accounts for around a quarter of all UK mammal species, there are more than 1,300 different species of bats worldwide, with more being discovered. Bat species in the UK are in decline due to habitat and food loss, excessive night lighting, urbanisation with its inherent risks of tall buildings and roads severing their travel routes, and cat attacks.

What do bats eat?

Primarily, British bats eat insects. They find their food using echolocation, and are incredibly accurate and manoeuvrable fliers. A common pipistrelle bat can eat up to 3,000 insects in a single night, which keeps the populations of insects such as midges and mosquitoes under control and also reduces the pest threat to crops. It also follows that as insect populations continue to fall, the survival of bats is threatened.

Where do bats live?

Although bats will sometimes roost in houses, some prefer to live in hollow trees or caves, and others live underground. Bats move to different roosts throughout the year, depending on the season. During the phases of pregnancy and nursing their young, female bats gather together in maternity roosts.

Some bats are protected species, and cannot be disturbed if discovered in a building. If you think you have bats living in your house, you can call the National Bat Helpline, run by the charity the Bat Conservation Trust.

How can we help bats?

• Have an open compost heap – this will attract more insects than a closed heap so the bats can feast on them at night.

• Put up bat boxes for roosts.

• Larger gardens could include some linear features such as hedges, which will help bats navigate.

• Choose plants to attract lots of insects to the garden, including night-flowering species to encourage nocturnal insects, to provide food for the bats.

• Put in a pond.

• Leave dead trees standing where it is safe to do so, and allow the garden to be a little wilder.

• Remove all external lighting.

• Keep cats shut in at night-time.

• Support farmers who practise methods that don't include pesticide sprays – widespread insect decimation means less food for bats. Other threats from large-scale agriculture includes hedgerow destruction, because bats use hedges for roosting and navigation.

▼ If there is no suitable natural roosting site you could try building a nesting box. Place it at least 3m (10 feet) from the ground in a spot that gets at least 6–8 hours of sunlight a day.

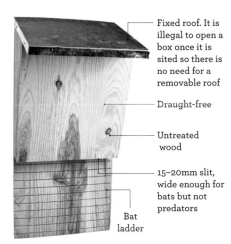

Fixed roof. It is illegal to open a box once it is sited so there is no need for a removable roof

Draught-free

Untreated wood

15–20mm slit, wide enough for bats but not predators

Bat ladder

Are parakeets here for good?

LARGE FLOCKS OF PARAKEETS are now common in London and the south-east of England, as well as in other parts of Europe. Are they an invasive species? How do they affect native species? Will they continue to spread, or might they die out?

The rose-ringed parakeet (also known as the ring-necked parakeet) is the only parrot living in the UK. It has become established in the Greater London area and Surrey, living in large noisy flocks which began to be big enough to get noticed in the 1980s and have spread rapidly and widely in the last 20 years. How they came to be in London is unknown – there are many urban myths as to how they arrived – but the first sightings were actually nearly 100 years earlier. They live on a variety of foods, including seeds, berries and scraps, and will visit a bird table.

Taking advantage of the warmth of the city and surrounding countryside – London has a large proportion of green space; it is designated a National Park City – parakeets are almost as common as pigeons. Although a tropical bird native to Africa and Asia they can cope with the colder winters in temperate countries, and as the climate continues to warm, parakeet sightings are likely further north and outside of cities.

Parakeets are secondary users of old woodpecker nest holes and similar spaces for breeding, which puts them in direct competition with the

Yes, it seems likely that the parakeets are a permanent visitor to the south of England. They are an adaptable species, and while still relatively alien to Britain and Europe, they show that wildlife can live successfully in an urban setting, and thrive because of climate change.

Nuthatch and bats. They are also fast, agile and visit feeding sites in flocks, so can outcompete other species for food. Debate still rages as to whether they are welcome or not in our skies.

UK government scientists acknowledge that the chance to eradicate the birds has now passed; there are simply too many of them. However, parakeets can be controlled under a licence where there is a localised threat to native ecosystems, crops or air safety. Parakeets are classified as a 'species of concern' for the European Union, but have not been designated as invasive – nonetheless, in June 2016, it was

◀ Exotic parakeets are now a common sight in the parks of London and around the south-east of England.

estimated there were around 85,000 rose-ringed parakeets in mainland Europe, and their numbers continue to increase.

A lesson has been learned, though, and related species, such as monk parakeets, have been culled and had their nests removed in a more-or-less successful attempt to eradicate them in the wild in the UK before the population gets too large (Greece is also attempting to control them).

FLYING IN: HOW DID PARAKEETS GET HERE?

Parakeets are not migratory birds, and although they are now widely distributed through Europe and southern Britain, it seems that they did not spread gradually from their native habitats. Rather they are escapees and, as common pets, this has meant that they have had the chance to colonise various European cities. In Greece, the first sightings were around Athens airport, in London in the 1890s parakeets were initially spotted around the docks. It is also likely that birds have escaped from domestic houses and zoos over the years. A variety of urban myths have gained popularity. For example, it is said that Jimi Hendrix released a pair in the 1970s, that a number of birds escaped from the film set of the *African Queen* in the 1950s, or even that they were escapee pets of King Henry VIII.

Can I leave a legacy, gardening-wise?

YOU WANT TO GARDEN to make a long-lasting difference to the environment, not just something to enjoy today. What can you do today to make the world better tomorrow?

Everyone can make a difference and whether it's creating a biodiverse, future-proofed wildlife garden, planting trees or making a community garden, there are plenty of ways gardeners can help future generations and the planet.

Trees

There is a Greek proverb that says a society grows great when old men plant trees whose shade they know they will never sit in. Planting a tree is a gift for the generations to come – it might be in your garden, an allotment, a community garden or on a street, but trees are the greatest legacy a gardener can leave.

Trees not only store carbon, they are homes for wildlife, they can foster woodland plant species and also help with preventing soil erosion and improving water quality, so it's important to choose the right tree for the place and not plant a random tree for the sake of it. To help choose the appropriate species, use a tool such as the RHS Plant Selector.

Cherry tree
Prunus spp.

If you can't plant any more trees in your garden or locally, consider making a donation to a charity or organisation that will plant them on your behalf. For example, Plant for the Planet – a campaign run by children and supported by the UN – aims to plant enough trees to offset the world's carbon emissions while the grown-ups are still arguing about what to do; it has already planted more than 13 billion trees.

Planting in the community

To contribute to the fabric of society as well as the environment, helping maintain or – better still – create community gardens and green spaces can have a lasting impact on a neighbourhood. Get together with other local people to instigate urban wildflower meadows, more street trees and convert scrubland to gardens and you will be beneftting the area for years to come.

Your own patch

How you manage your own plot will make a difference, and to leave a legacy of a biodiverse garden and a healthy ecosystem it is key to ensure you are gardening in the most sustainable way. Encourage wildlife and choose plants that will cope or even thrive in a changing climate so that your garden is more likely to survive the new potential conditions. That oft-repeated quote of Audrey Hepburn is true: 'To plant a garden is to believe in tomorrow.'

Spread the word

Gardening legacies can be an investment in plants, or they can be an investment in people. Getting younger generations interested in gardening will ensure there are horticulturalists in the future, both professional and amateur. Teach them how to plant trees and gardens so they can also make a physical difference. Similarly, starting a gardening group to foster horticultural knowledge as well as friendships and links between local people – and create new gardens – will not only gift the environment a greener future, but also the benefit the people of your community.

POSITIVE CHANGE IN THE WIDER WORLD

Voting with our wallets and supporting organisations and businesses that are working in a sustainable way to create a better future, such as organic farmers, is one way to effect changes that will hopefully lead to a better world. You could also start a campaign for local government to make positive changes for wildlife and the environment in your area, or for your children's school to teach more about gardening and nature. Alternatively, volunteer with charities whose work you admire.

Getting children interested in gardening and its rewards from an early age will set them up for a life of engagement with the natural world.

Chapter 2

How to Start Green

What is the most environmentally friendly way to arrange my garden?

REARRANGING YOUR SPACE can bring huge rewards, and it doesn't have to be hard. Keep in mind what you want out of your garden, and what kinds of wildlife you might want to attract. But is it a case of 'the more the merrier' when it comes to wildlife gardening? Or is it better to keep things simple?

Think about your garden as a habitat both for you *and* for wildlife. Get to know where the sunny spots are as well as any sheltered or shady nooks. That way you'll be able to make sure that bird boxes, bug hotels, log piles and your garden chairs are all sited where they'll get the most use.

Buddleia
Buddleja davidii

We've all seen it, a forlorn-looking patio built in a shady spot where no-one wants to sit. Or a worn patch running through a lawn where a path should be... Design mistakes like these are common, but they can be fixed. Re-evaluating your space is a useful exercise; try doing it after you come back from holiday so you can see your garden with fresh eyes.

While you're fixing things for the garden's human users, why not consider wildlife too? However, it pays to prioritise, especially in a small garden, where you might not be able to fit in a log pile, a wildlife pond *and* a wildflower meadow. Pick a few key features and work with those.

Really get to know your garden. Look at where the sunny spots are during the day and at different times of year. This will give you an idea of

HOW TO SKETCH OUT YOUR GARDEN

Drawing your ideas out on paper can be handy. Buy an extra-long measuring tape from a DIY store and measure out your garden. Be sure to note down the position of doors, windows, gates, trees and any drain covers. Use triangulation (measure between opposite corners) to ensure your plan is accurate.

Draw out your garden on graph paper – for most gardens 1:50 scale works well (2cm (¾ in) on paper equals 1m (3 ft) on the ground). Once you have all the immovable things plotted, it's time to have some fun!

Lay tracing paper over the top of your plan and start sketching out your ideas. Make sure you measure ideas from your graph paper and scale them up to life size to make sure they'll work. It's easy to get carried away and end up planning lots of features only to find you don't have the space.

Simplicity is key: it's best to do a few things well than lots of things badly. Give your human and wildlife habitats enough room so everyone can enjoy them.

good places for garden seats *and* where to position bee hotels, which need to face a southerly direction. If you're not sure which way is south, most mobile phones now have a compass tool.

Bird boxes are best on an east- or north-facing wall, so they'll avoid overheating in midday summer sun and escape westerly gales. Cooler, shadier areas of ground can be good places to make a log pile, build a shed or grow woodland flowers. Think of your garden as a series of different habitats for people, plants and wildlife.

◢ Insect hotels can provide valuable real estate for a range of creatures including solitary bees, which are useful pollinators of fruit bushes.

Am I stuck with my soil?

STUCK IN THE MUD. Grounded. Soil might seem like the most unchangeable thing in a garden, but are there ways to revitalise it? Can you turn stodgy clay into a lovely crumbly tilth? What effect will trying to improve your soil have on wildlife?

Soil is a miraculous substance. A single teaspoon of healthy garden soil contains more living things than there are people on the planet. When it's functioning well it's teeming with fungi, invertebrates and beneficial bacteria.

It might seem strange, but to function well, soil needs air. Air spaces within the soil allow breathing space for plant roots and soil wildlife.

Any soil can be improved by adding organic matter such as homemade compost or farmyard manure. Use mulches to protect the soil and try to sort out any compaction problems as soon as you spot them. By caring for and feeding the soil in this way you'll bring it to life and your plants and garden will be all the healthier for it.

Healthy topsoil is actually only about 50 – 70 per cent soil: the rest is made up of tiny pores and channels filled either with air or water.

When soil becomes compacted, these spaces are squished out and the soil becomes lifeless. Compaction is a common problem, especially on clay soils. Heavy machinery and people walking on bare soil are some of the main causes; it's a particular feature in new-build houses. Digging or forking the soil over is the quickest way to relieve compaction.

The key to improving your soil is to add organic matter such as garden compost (either homemade or from council waste collections) or well-rotted farmyard manure. You can either dig it in, or spread as a mulch and allow worms to incorporate it for you.

Sorting out your soil might seem like hard work, but any effort you put in will reap rich rewards. Adding organic matter such as compost is key.

POLLINATOR-FRIENDLY GREEN MANURES

Growing green manures is a great way to improve your soil. It's cheap and very effective. The basic idea is that you dig over your soil, scatter the seed and watch the flowers grow, before digging the plants in. This provides a low-cost, very environmentally friendly way of improving your soil. No financial or carbon costs of transporting compost or manure, and no plastic.

Generally the advice is to dig the plants in before they flower, but if you allow some to bloom, they're a great food source for pollinating insects such as bees and butterflies.

Phacelia (*Phacelia tanacetifolia*) A star bee plant. Pretty, fern-like leaves and blue flowers. Self-seeds readily but it's very easy to pull up if it appears where you don't want it.

Crimson clover (*Trifolium incarnatum*) Fixes nitrogen into the soil for an added boost of fertility. Deep rooted, so good at breaking up compacted soils. Rich red flowers in summer.

Mustard (*Sinapis alba*) Has 'biofumigant' properties so can prevent or discourage pests and diseases. Leave some patches to flower in mild spells in autumn and early spring.

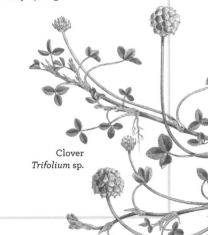

Clover
Trifolium sp.

Woodchip and chipped bark are the gardener's secret weapon when it comes to improving soil. Used as a mulch they provide a spongy layer that prevents further compaction when you walk on it. They feed all sorts of fungi and invertebrates as they break down, adding a long-lasting source of carbon, which is one of the engines of soil biodiversity.

Buying in soil is an option, but it can have high costs both financially and ecologically. There is a risk of contamination (broken glass and perennial weeds such as thistles are common contaminants), so if you do have to buy in soil, be sure to ask for a sample and check where it has come from.

Q Why doesn't my earth have earthworms?

Worms are a sign of healthy soil. They are also an important part of the food chain, supporting lots of wildlife. So what does it mean if your soil has no worms? And what can you do about it?

A Worms like cool, moist conditions and plenty of organic matter. Encourage worms into your garden by applying generous mulches of compost, shredded garden prunings, bark chippings or farmyard manure. Try to minimise digging as this disturbs worms and makes them more vulnerable to predators. Avoid using garden chemicals, especially fungicides, as these can affect earthworms too.

Mulching your soil with organic materials such as shredded garden prunings or chipped bark helps keep soil healthy and encourages worms.

What worms need

The answer to this question is, strangely enough, similar to what plant roots need: soil that contains air and water, and some organic matter. Organic matter simply means something that was once alive, in the garden context this generally means compost (either home-made or bought in from municipal waste schemes), fallen leaves or well-rotted farmyard manure. Sometimes you'll see bags of 'soil conditioner' or 'soil improver' for sale; these are generally a mix of one or more of these.

Shredded garden prunings, woodchip and chipped bark can all provide soil with organic matter, once they have rotted down a bit. They are especially useful as mulches: a layer of material applied on top of the soil. This helps keep the soil cool and moist, which is perfect for worms. Aim for a layer at least 5cm (2 in) deep.

Worms are sensitive to pesticides, especially fungicides, so avoid using them if you want to encourage worms into your garden. Cultivation (i.e. digging) also harms worms, destroying their burrows and leaving them vulnerable to predators. Unless your soil is badly compacted, put the spade away and let the worms do the work for you.

EARTHWORM INVASION! INTERNATIONAL WORMS AND WORLDWIDE WORMS

Worms are on the move across the world. In the USA and Canada, non-native European and Asian worms are invading the northern forests where there are no indigenous earthworms (they were all wiped out in the last Ice Age). Exotic worms – mainly brought in as fishing bait or with imported plants – are causing big problems, altering soils and ecosystems. Plants and animals have not adapted to the arrival of earthworms, and many are suffering.

Meanwhile back in the UK we've got our own worm woes. The New Zealand flatworm was accidentally introduced in the 1960s and has been causing problems ever since. It is a gruesome predator of our native earthworms, and in some places has severely reduced the populations. It's most common in cooler, wetter areas such as Scotland, northern England and Northern Ireland.

Flatworms eat earthworms by wrapping their bodies around them and dissolving them in digestive mucus. Flatworms hide in similar places to slugs; especially under pieces of wood or stones, and will often curl up like a Swiss roll. There are no chemical controls available, so the best means of dealing with them is to encourage their predators, such as rove beetles. Or squash them! If you pick them up, use rubber gloves as their coating of mucus can be a skin irritant.

Rove beetle
Staphylinidae

I've hardly any space: what can I grow?

SHORT ON SPACE BUT BIG ON IDEAS? It's a familiar situation for many gardeners. Don't worry, there's lots you can achieve, even if it's just on a balcony. Successful gardens and garden designs tend to focus around one key idea. Is it growing healthy organic food for your family? Or perhaps it's providing as many wildlife habitats as possible?

The best thing you can do when you're faced with a tiny garden is to decide what the main thing you want it to do is, and work from that. A strong sense of purpose brings with it meaning and will strengthen your plot's impact both visually and environmentally.

Almost anything is possible in a small garden, the key to success is to prioritise. Don't try to do too much. You might not have room for a wildflower meadow but you can still grow pots brimming with flowers for pollinators and put up a bug hotel. Every little bit really does help!

Grow to eat

Growing your own food is a great environmental gardening strategy. In a small garden, consider growing crops such as salad leaves or tomatoes in pots. And grow vertically. Thornless blackberries make a great climber for walls and fences and will give you a crop even in shady gardens. Dwarf or wall-trained fruit trees are another way of making use of vertical space.

Tomatoes grow brilliantly in pots and containers: once you've tasted your first homegrown harvest there's no going back!

GREEN ROOFS: FOR SHED, BIKE SHED OR BIN STORE!

Making a green roof is a great way to get the maximum value out of your outside space, and it doesn't need to be big. It is brilliant for disguising a bin store, an existing garden shed or a bike shelter, and can provide a useful source of nectar for pollinating insects. Green roofs can also improve air quality and help prevent flooding by slowing down rainwater run-off.

First things first, you need to make sure the structure is strong enough to support the weight of your green roof. They can be surprisingly heavy; even lightweight options can weigh as much as two bags of cement per square metre when saturated with rainfall.

The easiest option for mini green roofs is to buy ready-grown sedum matting (often referred to as 'sedum blanket'). This will already have a layer of substrate (the equivalent of soil) for the plants to grow in, along with a fleecy protection layer. The matting can simply be rolled out over a waterproof membrane such as a butyl pond liner on top of your existing roof. Sedum is the perfect green roof plant: it's low-growing, easy to care for, evergreen and it has flowers that bees and butterflies love.

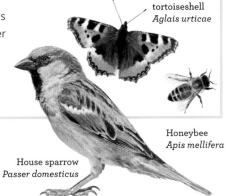

Small tortoiseshell
Aglais urticae

Honeybee
Apis mellifera

House sparrow
Passer domesticus

Grow for wildlife

There are several star plants for a small-scale wildlife garden. Make use of walls and fences by planting climbers, they give lots of value for very little space on the ground. Ivy is a particularly useful one as its flowers are great for late-flying pollinators and its evergreen growth provides shelter for birds and all kinds of other creatures.

If you can fit in a small tree, crab apples have fantastic wildlife credentials and they look great too. Their pretty spring blossom is a magnet for bees and their colourful autumn and winter fruits are a valuable source of food for birds.

Should my paving come up?

OVER A QUARTER of all front gardens are now entirely paved over. But what effect is this having on the natural world – and us? What's the best way to create a green oasis in a concrete desert?

Too much paving is bad news both for wildlife and human wellbeing. Any paving that you can remove and replace with planting will have a positive impact, and there are lots of plants that will grow brilliantly in the newly revealed spaces. For help and ideas, get involved with the RHS Greening Great Britain campaign: rhs.org.uk/ggb.

Keeping your outdoor space green has multiple benefits for both our physical and mental health – not to mention for wildlife too.

Paving the way to disaster

The proliferation of paving in Britain in recent years has been bad news for both people and wildlife. It's estimated that in London an area 22 times the size of Hyde Park has been paved over in recent years. That's a lot of bird-friendly hedges, buzzing borders and luxuriant lawns turned into grey wasteland.

Paving over gardens doesn't just affect wildlife, it affects people too. Seeing greenery is proven to lift a person's mood and has a beneficial effect on mental health and wellbeing. Physical health is improved too: hedges and trees trap pollution, preventing it from entering your

FOUR WAYS TO TURN GREY TO GREEN

Lift a slab and plant a tree
Small trees such as rowans
(*Sorbus*), flowering cherries
(*Prunus*), juneberries (*Amelanchier*)
and crab apples (*Malus*) can easily
be planted in the space left by a
standard paving slab. For best
results plant trees in late autumn
or early winter.

Plant the gaps If there are wide
mortar gaps between old paving
slabs, scrape the cement out and
fill with soil. Plant dwarf creeping
or alpine plants, such as thymes
(*Thymus* – be sure to pick creeping
varieties like 'Bressingham Pink'),
mind-your-own-business (*Soleirolia
soleirolii*) or Corsican mint
(*Mentha requienii*).

Plant a climber Even if you only
have a very narrow strip of soil
next to the house, plant a climber.
It will give you a lot of value
without taking up much room
at ground level. If you pick a
self-clinging climber like climbing
hydrangea, ivy or campsis
you won't even need to
provide support.

If you really can't avoid having
hard surfaces, consider using
permeable paving. Although it
doesn't provide many wildlife or
wellbeing benefits, at least it is
less likely to contribute to flooding
problems. Resin-bonded gravel
or concrete lawn reinforcements
are two options.

home (and lungs). Greenery keeps
towns and cities cool in heatwaves.
It also slows down run-off rates by
up to 50 per cent and helps to absorb
floodwater during storms.

Juneberry
*Amelanchier
laevis*

What should I do with my old paving slabs?

If you're able to remove paving slabs
intact, they can be reused, for example
as a path in a greenhouse or as a base
for a shed. Alternatively, put them on
a local classifieds site so someone else
can re-use them, or take them to your
local recycling centre and put them
in the 'rubble' compartment.

Q Will my garden ever be perfectly green?

SO YOU'VE PUT IN YOUR WILDLIFE POND, sown a meadow and hung up bird feeders. Job done? Not quite. Gardens change over time, saplings grow into towering trees, sunny borders become shaded and wildlife moves in, out and through. Learning to embrace a garden's evolution is a valuable skill.

Viburnum opulus

Flower

Berrries

A As the Greek philosopher Heraclitus said: 'There is nothing permanent except change.' Gardens are living, breathing things and so will inevitably change over time. Accepting these changes and adapting to them is one of the secrets of being a successful gardener.

Viburnum opulus can outgrow its space as it grows to 8m (24 ft). Its fragrant flowers in spring are highly attractive to bees. The autumn red berries are loved by mistle thrushes and bullfinches. If the shrub grows too tall for your garden it will tolerate hard pruning.

When you're laying out a new design, digging over-compacted soil or labouring over your dream wildlife pond you might be longing to sit back and look lovingly over a 'finished' garden. However, reality is never that simple.

Gardens change over time, plants grow and the conditions they create are constantly changing. A garden full of young trees will be light and airy. A decade later as the canopies close over, some may need to be removed or thinned – unless you're aiming for a dark forest look!

Part of the delight of gardening is that you never know for certain how plants will grow. Sometimes they will grow almost too well, sometimes not enough. Casting a critical eye over things every now and then is a useful exercise. Don't be afraid to change things that aren't working, and do more of the things that work well for you and your garden's wildlife.

KEY THINGS TO LOOK OUT
FOR AS YOUR GARDEN MATURES

Do my trees and shrubs need pruning?

Often people assume that because a tree or shrub has outgrown its space it needs to be removed. Mature plants are really important for wildlife, so consider pruning them instead of removing them.

Do my plants need rejuvenating?

Perennial plants like daylilies, crocosmias and asters tend to become congested over time. Dig them up in autumn or early spring, divide and move them.

Have my hedges got out of control?

Unless you're very zealous with the trimmers, hedges – particularly privet – will get wider with time. Most can be trimmed back in early spring (but avoid working on them during the bird nesting season). Aim for a flat-topped 'A' shape to allow light to reach the bottom for even growth.

Have light levels changed?

Perhaps a tree you've planted has turned a sunny part of the garden into a shadier one, or a tree has been cut down. Either way, you'll need to adapt your planting.

Is my pond getting overgrown?

Ponds are a fertile environment, and aquatic plants can be fairly vigorous. After a few years, pretty much all wildlife ponds will need a bit of clearance to ensure there's still some open water.

Are my plants happy and healthy?

Sometimes plants will take a year or so to establish themselves. If after this time, they're not growing away happily, it's time to move them somewhere else or replace them.

Over time, hedges tend to become misshapen. Luckily most kinds respond well to hard pruning and will grow back bushier than ever.

Q Does double-digging help a neglected plot?

DOUBLE-DIGGING is a traditional technique that was mainly deployed in vegetable gardens. The idea is to enrich the soil as much as possible and break up any compaction below the surface. It's often considered unnecessary and a bit old-fashioned these days, but can it still have its uses?

Why bother?

The idea behind double-digging is to dig further down than normal so you break up any compaction and add organic matter (compost or manure) more deeply than would otherwise be possible.

This is particularly valuable if your soil has been compacted, for example by heavy machinery used during house building, or regular use of a rotavator on a vegetable patch can create a hard 'pan' just below where the blades reach. This compacted layer deters plant roots and stops moisture moving through the soil, making it more vulnerable to drought and flooding.

How to do it

Mark out a line using string and pegs. Dig the soil out to a spade's depth, placing it to one side. Fork over the bottom of your trench, adding compost or well-rotted manure. Move your line forward 60cm (2 ft) and dig another trench, backfilling the previous one. Repeat. Barrow the soil round from your first trench to fill the last one.

A

Double-digging can be worth doing if your soil has become compacted, especially in a new-build plot where the compacted soil may be hidden beneath a layer of imported topsoil. However, you're generally better off adding more organic matter to the soil surface and letting the worms and other wildlife do the work for you.

Is it worth doing?

If your soil is particularly poor and compacted, double-digging can be a useful way to kick-start a healthy garden. However, this amount of disturbance will temporarily suppress a lot of the life in the soil (everything from beneficial bacteria to mycorrhizal fungi and worms) so many gardeners prefer to add organic matter to the surface and let nature take its course.

Why don't birds visit my garden?

WHETHER IT IS THE MELODIC SONG of a blackbird or a cheeky robin following you round hoping for worms, birds bring joy to a garden. But what if you've put out the fat balls, peanuts, and even built a bird table, and your garden *still* seems to be missed by our feathered friends?

There are several reasons for a lack of feathered visitors to gardens, including time of year and a lack of suitable cover. Don't panic, plant some evergreen shrubs and climbers – and be patient!

Blue tit
*Cyanistes
caeruleus*

Most gardeners love to see birds, and gardens are an increasingly important habitat for many species. Some are valuable garden allies: blue tits, for example, love to devour aphids, and thrushes eat snails.

Provide cover

Most of the birds we're used to seeing in gardens are fairly low down in the food chain, so they spend their lives on the lookout for predators ready to devour them. Evergreen shrubs and climbers are especially valuable hiding places.

BIRD-FRIENDLY GARDEN FEATURES

Bird feeders Place feeders out of the reach of cats, and ideally close to a source of cover. Feed all year and clean them regularly.

Dense, berry-bearing evergreen shrubs (especially *Pyracantha*) These provide valuable cover and nesting sites for birds (see pp. 84).

Climber-covered wall or fence (especially ivy) A perfect place for birds to hide and perhaps nest too.

Bird boxes Different boxes suit different species. Fix them at least 2m (6 ft) high on walls, fences and in trees.

Which features will make my garden greener?

THERE'S SO MUCH ADVICE on eco-friendly gardening, it can be difficult to know where to start. Should you rush out and invest in lots of bug and bird boxes? Or is it best to take a look at what your garden can achieve in a broader sense?

▷ Ponds are one of the greenest features going, and allow you to grow beautiful aquatic plants too.

White water lily
Nymphaea alba

Putting in a pond is generally considered to be the single most effective way to boost your garden's wildlife credentials. And almost any plant will be better for the environment than a paving slab; small, flowering trees such as crab apples or rowans have particularly strong eco-credentials.

'Ecosystem services' is a relatively new term. It describes what plants and gardens can do in a broad sense to help our environment; from providing habitats for wildlife to helping fight the causes and effects of climate change.

Our gardens can be a hugely valuable force for good. Think about all your garden features and how you can maximise their ecosystem services. Perhaps a shed could have a green roof to provide nectar for pollinating insects. If you're going to plant a tree to give you some privacy from the neighbours, why not make it a bee-friendly tree?

Best garden features for ecosystem services

Ponds – bring in all manner of specialised aquatic life, plus birds and mammals will come to drink. The insects they support can become an important source of food for birds and bats.

Hedges – help cut pollution, support wildlife, and can even help prevent flooding by slowing down water run-off during downpours. Plant a mixed hedge of several different types of plant to maximise wildlife value.

CURRENT CONCERNS AND HOW GARDENERS CAN HELP TACKLE THEM

Reduce plastic use Grow your own fruit and veg, especially those which are easy to grow yet difficult to buy without plastic wrapping, such as salads. Re-use plant pots or take them to garden centre recycling schemes.

Help bees Grow a bee-friendly tree. Besides being great for wildlife and the environment, some trees are absolute winners when it comes to supporting bees. Crab apples, rowans, the Indian bean tree (*Catalpa bignonioides*) and the bee-bee tree (*Tetradium daniellii*) are all star players here.

Cut carbon footprint Studies have shown that growing evergreen climbers on house walls acts as insulation, keeping your home warmer in winter and cooler in summer. One study showed an almost 40 per cent reduction in energy consumption on ivy-covered surfaces.

Sunflower
Helianthus spp.

Meadows – let even just a part of your lawn grow longer and it will come alive with butterflies, bees and more. Plus you'll save fuel (reducing your carbon footprint) and time by leaving the lawnmower in the shed. Trim the edges and a pathway through for a smarter, more 'intentional' look.

Borders – can be a year-round larder for wildlife. Birds love feasting on berries from shrubs such as cotoneasters and berberis, along with seeds from sunflowers and teasels. Look for the RHS Plants for Pollinators logo for bee- and butterfly-friendly plants.

Q Is it okay to buy compost?

ENVIRONMENTALLY SPEAKING, nothing beats homemade compost. It's also generally the cheapest option. But what if you don't have any, or the compost you have just isn't ready to use yet? Is it okay to buy some in? And is homemade compost suitable for all kinds of garden uses?

Making your own compost is a brilliant way to use up kitchen and garden waste, and to boost your soil's health and fertility. It also comes with good climate credentials too; by preventing waste entering landfill it means your waste won't end up producing lots of methane, which is a potent greenhouse gas. Not only that but there's a carbon boost too, as homemade compost helps keep carbon in the soil rather than escaping into the atmosphere.

However, home-made compost isn't always the answer. In a new garden, you may simply not have enough material to make a useful amount of compost. More is definitely more when it comes to the poor soil found around many new-build houses: they'll soak up all the compost you can give them.

Certain other situations merit buying in compost. Sowing seeds for example; homemade compost is alive with fungi, insects and weed seeds; great for the garden but bad news for delicate seedlings under cover. If you want to grow ericaceous (acid-soil-loving) plants like

A Homemade compost is generally better for the environment, better for your garden and cheaper than store-bought bags. However, bought-in composts are useful when you're sowing seeds or growing specialist plants like orchids, cacti and ericaceous species like blueberries. Always look for peat-free.

blueberries, but your garden soil isn't acid, then grow them in containers of ericaceous compost. This is difficult to mix at home, so buy in a proprietary peat-free ericaceous mix.

Blueberry
Vaccinium

What about peat?

Peat is an incredibly precious natural resource. Peat bogs help fight climate change by absorbing CO_2 from the atmosphere, hold water and support a range of wonderful wildlife; by choosing peat-free composts you're helping the environment in a big way.

If your local garden centre or DIY store doesn't stock peat-free compost, write to them and ask them why not.

▶ Avoid peat-based compost at all costs as it has a negative environmental impact.

WHAT'S IN THE BAG?

Remember, unless your bag of compost says 'peat-free' then it probably isn't. Many composts are now 'peat-reduced,' which is at least a start.

Multipurpose Traditional 'multipurpose' composts are almost entirely peat, with a little fertiliser and lime added. Nowadays they are increasingly peat-free or peat-reduced. It may take a bit of careful reading of the packaging to work this out. Mainly used for potting-on plants, although sometimes they can also be suitable for seed sowing (especially larger seeds). 'Multipurpose' is a misnomer, don't dig these composts into your garden soil.

Seed and cutting compost A finer grade of multipurpose, which will have been sieved to give a smaller particle size, to help avoid swamping delicate seedlings.

Contains low levels of fertiliser, as seeds and cuttings don't need as many nutrients in their early stages.

Specialist composts (orchids, cacti, ericaceous) Some plants need very particular soil conditions and there is a range of composts available to suit them. Generally it's not worth mixing your own so these are worth buying if you want to grow such plants; just make sure the compost is peat-free.

Soil improver or soil conditioner Generally a mix of rotted farmyard manure with varying percentages of municipally composted green waste and sometimes composted bark too. As the name suggests these are designed to be spread or dug into the garden soil, and won't be suitable for pot plants or seedlings.

What helps the environment more – flowers or vegetables?

FOR THE ECO-MINDED GARDENER, it can seem like a tough decision. Do you go for edibles with all their environmental and health benefits, or choose flowers for their beauty and wildlife value? Is one better than the other? Or can you have both?

Both edible crops and ornamental flowers can have great value for the eco-minded gardener. Grow them using sustainable methods and the rewards for you (and the earth) will be rich. If you can't decide between veg or flowers, remember that there are lots of ornamental yet edible plants that have wildlife value too. Every garden and gardener is different; grow what's right for you.

Why is growing your own 'green'?

About 30 per cent of all greenhouse gas emissions are related to the food we buy. Meat and dairy are by far the biggest culprits. Fruit and veg have a much smaller (although still notable) impact. Transport, processing, packaging, waste and the use

Chamomile flowers

of chemical fertilisers all play a part in this – and it can be largely avoided if you grow your own.

Home-grown produce also helps us side-step a host of other environmental issues that can crop up when fruit and veg are grown a long way from home. Water diverted away from local people and wildlife to feed thirsty crops for export is a big problem in some areas. And of course there's the inevitable scourge of plastic pollution that comes from both growing and packaging crops. Growing your own salad leaves is especially valuable in this respect.

What about flowers?

Flowers from the garden can have some pretty impressive eco-credentials too. Cut-flower production overseas can be environmentally problematic, with reports of excess chemical use and abuses of workers' rights, alongside questions of water and land use and the climate implications of airfreighting crops over such large distances. This can make a home-grown bouquet sound all the more appealing.

PLANT SUPERSTARS: FRUIT AND VEG WITH FLOWER POWER

Leeks: Leave a leek or two to flower and you'll see that they're closely related to the oh-so-fashionable ornamental alliums. Bees couldn't care less about fashion but they absolutely adore leek flowers.

Kale: Another plant that reveals its family history when it runs to seed. If you let a few plants flower at the end of the season you'll be rewarded with mountains of bright yellow, rapeseed-like flowers. These smell like honey and are a big hit with pollinators.

Cardoons & artichokes: These attractive, aristocratic veg make striking additions to a flower border. Grow some spare plants and let them bloom away happily without being harvested. Bumblebees in particular adore

Lavender
Lavandula sp.

their huge, pollen-rich violet flowers.

Fruit trees: Peaches, plums and apricots are great for early blossom, which is joyful to look at and a lifesaver for many different early-flying bees. Apples and pears also look wonderful in bloom and are a superb resource for pollinators.

Herbs: Many herbs are wildlife magnets. Cultivated oregano and marjoram are close cousins of their wildflower equivalents and are particularly loved by butterflies. Lavender, hyssop, thyme, rosemary, spearmint and even bay laurel all make it onto the RHS Plants for Pollinators lists.

Choose your flowers carefully and wildlife will make a bee-line for your garden. Supporting pollinating insects is an obvious win from growing flowers. By selecting RHS Plants for Pollinators plants (see rhs.org.uk/plantsforpollinators) you can be sure that your flowers will be great for bees, butterflies and a host of other welcome garden visitors.

Don't get too worried about picking the 'right' thing though. Growing anything is better than nothing, and there's no definitive right answer about what you should grow in your garden.

Mint
Mentha sp.

Can planting be too dense for wildlife?

DENSE, LUSH GROWTH IN GARDENS is generally thought of as a good thing for wildlife. Plenty of hiding places, and plenty of flowers to visit. But is this true for all wildlife? Are there some creatures that appreciate a bit of bare earth?

Plum
*Prunus
domestica*

Think of a wildlife garden and you'll probably think of a green, exuberant place overflowing with flowers, trees and shrubs. Think of a bee and you'll probably think of a bustling little honeybee that lives in a hive. Both of these images show only part of the bigger picture.

Having a richly planted garden is the most eco-friendly approach. However, some creatures do enjoy access to open areas so don't be tempted to cram your entire plot completely full. Try to strike a balance between planting and spaces between for maximum benefit; as an added bonus, some of the ground-nesting bees you'll attract are fantastic pollinators for fruit and veg crops.

Honeybees are just one of about 270 different species of bee that call the UK home. We have mining bees, mason bees, leafcutter bees and even hairy-footed flower bees! Many of these are ground-nesting and appreciate areas of bare soil. They'll often nest in paths or in threadbare patches on short lawns.

One giveaway sign of ground-nesting bees is small 'volcanoes' of fine soil particles on your lawn. Don't worry, it won't hurt the grass and the mining bees that live in them are very unlikely to sting humans.

Open, sunny areas without too much vegetation are also attractive to lizards and slow worms; these cold-blooded reptiles appreciate basking spots where they can soak up the sun and warm their bodies. So don't fret if your garden isn't wall-to-wall flowers: even bare earth has its uses.

GROUND-NESTING BEES

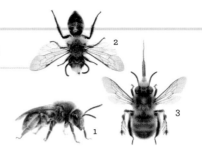

Many of our native bees like to nest underground. Some bumblebees nest in existing cavities, such as mouse burrows, while other species like the mining bees are – as their name suggests – excavation specialists. These wild bees can be excellent pollinators for a range of garden crops including raspberries, apples and tomatoes. Spring and early summer is the best time to spot them.

1. Orange-tailed mining bee, also known as the early mining bee (*Andrena haemorrhoa*) A frequent garden visitor. Has a black abdomen and a furry orange bottom.

2. Ashy mining bee (*Andrena cineraria*) Sometimes forms large 'colonies' (although each nest is separate and contains only one female. Females are black with two bands of ash-grey fur.

3. Hairy-footed flower bee (*Anthophora plumipes*) As the name suggests, this is a pretty hirsute bee, with crazy-looking plumes of hair along its legs. Darts about quickly and loves deadnettles in particular.

4. Tawny mining bee (*Andrena fulva*) A distinctive, bright orange bee; look out for these on your gooseberry and currant bushes. Nests are vertical shafts 20 to 30cm (8–12 in) deep.

5. Red mason bee (*Osmia bicornis*) This common bee nests in a range of sites including bee hotels and bare soil and needs access to bare areas of mud to seal up its nest chambers. A very useful pollinator.

Raspberry
Rubus idaeus

QAre wildflowers best?

IF YOU WANT TO BRING WILDLIFE INTO THE GARDEN, should you be planting wildflowers? Is a wildflower the same as a native flower? What does native mean anyway, and does it matter?

A Native plants and wildflowers are great for wildlife. However, non-native plants are important too, and the question of whether something is native or not will become increasingly irrelevant as our climate continues to change in the future.

▼ Many wildflowers such as this cornflower make charming, wildlife-friendly garden plants.

Cornflower
Centaurea cyanus

The term wildflower simply means 'uncultivated plants that grow without human intervention'. Often when we think of wildflowers we assume native plants, like primroses and cow parsley.

However, 'native' is something of an arbitrary term that varies around the world. In Britain, for example, a plant is generally considered native if it's been here since the end of the last Ice Age; while in Canada, plants are generally considered native if they grew there before European settlement began just a few hundred years ago.

Traditional definitions of nativeness also don't take into account the fact that nature changes over time, and natural habitats for a particular species might expand or contract. There's plenty of fossil evidence to show that hippos, elephants and even the dreaded *Rhododendron ponticum* used to be native to the British Isles, during warm periods between past Ice Ages.

Today, human-induced climate change is already speeding up species migration at an unprecedented rate. Alpine plants are heading higher and higher up mountains, and plants are growing closer to the poles than ever before. Effectively our gardens are heading south at a rate of 12m (40 ft) a day, so what was native 10,000 years ago might not be native anymore.

Recent examples of changing ranges of species include the tree bumblebee (*Bombus hypnorum*) and tongue orchids (*Serapias* spp.), both of which seem to have made it to Britain of their own accord. Sycamore (*Acer pseudoplatanus*) is a hotly debated plant, with some botanists arguing it could be called native as it would have got here eventually, while others list it as an invasive species to be cleared at all cost.

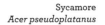

Sycamore
Acer pseudoplatanus

Yet sycamore has relatively good wildlife credentials and isn't as vulnerable to emerging pest and disease threats as some of our native trees. Should we be trying to eradicate it, along with the tree bumblebee (which coincidentally has excellent pollination abilities), just because they don't fit our definition of native? We're going to need to embrace more diversity in future, and climate change will only make this more urgent.

PLANTS FOR BUGS

The Royal Horticultural Society (RHS) conducted a survey to see whether insects prefer native plants. Gardens contain on average only 30 per cent native plants, so are gardeners missing a trick when it comes to wildlife?

During the four-year study, RHS scientists counted over 80,000 invertebrates representing more than 300 different species. The conclusion was that using native plants in your garden is helpful for some forms of wildlife, but that well-chosen non-native plants have plenty to offer too.

A mixture of native and non-native plants was found to be particularly helpful for pollinating insects, due to the fact that exotic plants help extend the flowering season in gardens. The study also showed that dense planting, but with a few bare patches of soil was best for wildlife in general.

To quote one of the scientists involved: 'Most importantly, any planting in a garden is better than none for invertebrates and diversity of plant origin in a garden is a strength, not a weakness.'

Can a garden be made green quickly?

IS THERE SUCH A THING AS 'INSTANT GARDENING'? Are there any shortcuts to making a garden look good, fast? How do you balance quick results with being eco-friendly?

▲ Growing seeds and cuttings (using biodegradable pots) is a green way to get more plants.

If you want to make a garden quickly, there are a number of techniques you can use to get it looking established pronto. It's a good idea to have a long-term plan and work towards it in stages. If you've set out your long-term plants, and spaced them so they have room to grow in the coming years, the garden can look a bit empty at first. Try using annual flowers (such as cosmos and cornflowers) as temporary fillers. They'll look great and the bees will thank you for it.

For a spectacular, quick, friendly and cheap garden feature, take the annual flowers idea one step further by sowing a 'pictorial meadow' mix. These plants can start flowering in as little as three months from seed, bringing swathes of glorious colour. You'll get months of wildlife-friendly flowers for not much money, although it will need to be re-sown each year.

Grow annual flowers, climbers and add a quick-growing shrub or two to get your garden off to a flying start. It's rarely worthwhile investing in large, ready-grown plants, and there are some good environmental reasons to avoid them. Smaller plants generally establish better and will soon grow away. Part of the joy of gardening is watching your space develop over time.

Buying big plants: what you need to know

It can be tempting to head out to the garden centre and buy some really big plants for instant impact. However, there are some good environmental and practical reasons not to do this.

Many large ready-grown plants will have been imported from abroad. This comes with a big carbon cost in terms of transport, and risks bringing in new

QUICK-GROWING PLANTS TO MAKE YOUR GARDEN LOOK GOOD ALMOST INSTANTLY

California lilac (*Ceanothus*) A superb group of quick-growing shrubs. Many are evergreen and all have blue or white flowers that are much loved by bees. Try 'concha', 'skylark' or 'autumnal Blue'.

Mallow (*Lavatera* x *clementii*, *L. maritima*) A shrubby relative of the hollyhock, grows really quickly into a flower-smothered shrub. A useful gap filler between slower-growing permanent plants. Great for dry, sunny gardens.

Miscanthus (*Miscanthus sinensis*) A huge grass that can get to 2m (6 ft) if conditions are right.

For impact it's hard to beat. Simply slice off all the growth in late winter – be sure to leave some out for the birds to use as nesting materials.

Honeysuckle (*Lonicera periclymenum*) A native flowering climber that's good for many creatures, especially birds and moths. Needs support, so provide an obelisk or trellis panel for its twining stems.

Honeysuckle
Lonicera periclymenum

pests and diseases. Generally, smaller plants will be able to adapt more quickly to conditions in your garden, and may well soon overtake larger bought-in ones anyway. Always choose British-grown wherever possible.

There are some plants it's never worth buying in larger pot sizes. Shrubby Mediterranean herbs such as lavenders are generally short-lived (especially in the cosy conditions of a plant nursery), so by buying large plants you're just getting something that won't live as long as a smaller, cheaper one.

Design tips
Add instant height with arches, obelisks in borders and trellis panels on fences. Locally sourced hazel rods are an environmentally-friendly construction material, and give a rustic charm. Plant plenty of climbers, many are quick growing and provide that all-important height that gives gardens an instant air of maturity. Honeysuckle, rambling roses and ivy are especially wildlife-friendly climbers.

Q How crucial is sunlight?

SUNLIGHT IS THE BASIC SOURCE OF ENERGY
for almost all life on earth, either directly or indirectly.
But does a wildlife garden have to be in a sunny spot?
Or can shady gardens have wildlife value too?

Plants are pretty incredible organisms. Using energy from sunlight they convert carbon dioxide, water and minerals from the soil into energy-rich compounds, including into the fruits, leaves, shoots, roots and seeds that we eat. This is accomplished via a process known as photosynthesis, and its by-product is oxygen. We have a lot to thank plants for!

So sunlight is pretty important overall. But how much do plants need, and do they all need the same amount? In full leaf, the trees in a forest can gobble up more than 90 per cent of the sunlight before it hits the forest floor. Yet deciduous woodlands can be full of plants and wildlife at ground level.

If your garden is shady, don't fight it: choose woodland plants like ferns, primroses and bluebells, which are adapted to grow in lower light levels. Ivy is a great shade plant and is really useful for a range of different insects and birds. Focus on attracting woodland wildlife such as beetles, bats and woodpeckers. Why not continue the woodland theme by creating a log pile too?

Broomrape
Orobanche

Vampire plants

A few plants refuse to play nicely and don't bother to use sunlight for themselves at all. Some are parasitic, such as broomrapes (*Orobanche*) and toothworts (*Lathraea*), latching on to their host's roots to steal nutrients. Purple toothwort (*Lathraea clandestina*) can sometimes be seen growing wild on the roots of willows, poplars and alders.

A Almost all plants need at least some sunlight to grow; however there are many that cope with quite a lot of shade. Sheltered shady corners can be a great habitat for all sorts of creatures. Go for a woodland theme and you won't go far wrong!

Can I conquer builders' rubble?

NEW-BUILD HOUSES OFTEN COME with a whole load of trouble just below the surface. Leftover rubble is often accidentally compacted into the soil or hidden by a thin layer of imported topsoil. What's the best way to go from muddy mess to blooming borders?

Finding rubble can be an annoying hindrance, but it definitely doesn't doom your garden forever. Removing it before you lay out your garden is the best option, but you can easily build the soil up instead. It all depends on how much time you have and how long you plan on living in the house.

DISPOSING OF RUBBLE

Rubble can be a useful source of hardcore for future building projects, such as garden steps. Broken tiles, bricks and pipes can make an interesting and wildlife-friendly filling for gabions. If you need to get rid of it entirely, take it to your local household recycling centre or pay someone licensed to dispose of it.

The thorough way to deal with rubble

A belt-and-braces approach to dealing with rubble is to divide the garden into patches and dig them over thoroughly in turn, removing unwanted rubbish as you find it. If you already have a design in mind, build your paths first so you can avoid trampling mud around. Then add as much soil conditioner as you can lay your hands on.

The cheat's way to deal with rubble

If you're not able to remove rubble, the best way to remedy the situation is to build the soil up. So use soil conditioners like municipal green waste compost or well-rotted farmyard manure. If the soil is compacted, fork them in. Generous mulches of woodchip or chipped bark will help build the soil profile over time.

Building rubble

Is a small tree better than no tree at all?

Is THERE REALLY such a thing as a small tree, or does every tree become big over time? Are all trees useful for wildlife? What other things can trees do? And are they hard work to care for?

Trees are our friends. Love them, hug them, plant them! Trees offer a huge number of wildlife benefits for very little work. There's a tree for almost any garden, no matter how small – and luckily some of the most wildlife-friendly ones are the prettiest too.

Trees matter. They give us the air we breathe, help protect us from floods and heatwaves, provide food and shelter for wildlife. In almost any garden, a tree is better than no tree!

Many gardeners worry about small trees gradually turning into giants, like the 'miniature' conifers in so many 1970s gardens that turned into green behemoths. Luckily there are lots of wildlife-friendly small trees that will never get taller than your house. Trees generally take very little work. They'll need watering in dry weather and staking in their first couple of years, after that it's mostly a case of removing the odd misplaced or damaged branch.

Tree-planting tips
Pot-grown trees can be planted at any time of year, but if you can, plant trees in autumn or early winter. This gives them plenty of time to grow new roots before the risk of summer drought.
1. Dig a hole slightly larger and very slightly deeper than the pot, put your tree in and replace the soil round the roots. Firm the soil gently, water in well and stake the tree if necessary.
2. A mulch of chipped bark for a 1m (3 ft) radius round the trunk is helpful to get the tree established.

Turn a shrub into a tree
A handy technique for getting a small tree that will never grow enormous is to train a shrub into a tree by 'crown lifting'. This works really well with any of the more vigorous California lilacs (*Ceanothus*), along with cherry laurel (*Prunus laurocerasus*), cotoneasters and smoke bushes (*Cotinus*). You can do this to an existing plant by cutting off the lower branches back to the trunk; or train a new plant, either as a multi-stemmed plant or the more traditional 'lollipop' shape.

FOUR OF THE BEST SMALL TREES FOR WILDLIFE

1. Amelanchiers Perhaps the perfect small tree. Amelanchiers are also known as juneberries or serviceberries; the name is a reference to their small but tasty fruits, which are adored by birds. Pretty spring blossom, delicate summer foliage and great autumn leaf colour. Recommended varieties include *Amelanchier lamarckii* and *A.* x *grandiflora* 'Robin Hill'.

2. Crab apples There are many cultivars of crab apples and they're all great for wildlife. Generous spring blossom – beloved by bees – is followed by small apples which provide a useful source of food for birds over the colder months. Recommended varieties include *Malus toringo* 'Scarlett', *Malus sylvestris* (our native crab apple) and *Malus* 'Evereste'.

3. Cotoneasters You might think of cotoneasters as shrubs, but some are big enough to be grown as small trees. *Cotoneaster* 'Cornubia' makes a superb, semi-evergreen tree that provides privacy for humans along with food and shelter for birds. White flowers in summer become vivid scarlet red autumn berries.

4. Hawthorns Our native hawthorns (*Crataegus monogyna* and *C. laevigata*) and their single-flowered cultivated varieties (such as 'Punicea') make great small garden trees. They have white or pink flowers in spring followed by red autumn fruits. Loved by birds, bees and butterflies.

Is a narrow garden still useful for wildlife?

HAVING A GARDEN that's more like a runway in shape is a common problem. Boxy fencing and straight concrete paths often make things worse. Can I still create an interesting, green garden without making the garden look smaller?

A typical strip garden has fences on both sides, a straight concrete path, lawns and not much else. They often feel much smaller than they really are because the eye shoots straight to the end, foreshortening the garden considerably. How, then, can one make the eye linger longer and appreciate the space for what it really is?

Shape it

Anything you can do to emphasise the width of your plot will make it feel bigger. Diagonals are useful; by lengthening lines going across the garden, they widen the perspective. Try diagonals in paving, borders or even topiary repeated across the garden. Circles are a great way to hold the eye, cut your lawn into a circle shape or lay a circular patio. Or combine both principles and put some sweeping curves into the design going from side to side.

Breaking boundaries

Disguise or break up the boundaries as much as possible. Climbers, shrubs and trees will help to hide unsightly

You can easily disguise the shape of a long narrow garden and make it feel more spacious by designing different shapes into it. Diagonals and circles work brilliantly to emphasise the width of a space. Break it up into separate garden 'rooms' and add in some height from climbers and archways, allowing views through, and you'll never know it was once a strip.

fences. By not being able to see exactly where the garden ends, your brain will perceive it to be bigger. Use trellis panels to support wildlife-friendly climbers, such as honeysuckle, and plant small trees, such as crab apples. They don't have to go right at the end or by the sides either, by having them closer to the house and being able to look through, under or around them, you'll help banish that boxed-in feeling.

Grow up!

Use vertical space to your advantage. While they do take up some room, trees, obelisks, archways, and shrubs pull the eye up and out, making the space seem larger. Small gardens don't need small features; if you miniaturise everything it will seem cramped and tiny. Select a few favourite features and make space to do them well.

Through the garden gate

Dividing a long, narrow plot into a series of 'rooms' is a tried-and-tested way of making the most of a strip garden. Each one can have its own feeling and perhaps be tailored to a particular kind of wildlife. The key to making this type of design work is to ensure there are always opportunities to see glimpses through to the next 'room'. Archways can be useful, or invite exploration with a curved path that leads out of sight.

Having different layers and heights in your garden also helps make it seem larger.

NARROW TREES FOR WILDLIFE

Narrow, columnar trees are useful in strip gardens as they give you height but take up very little space. Here are a few to try.

Sorbus aucuparia 'Fastigiata' An upright form of our native rowan

Hoheria 'Borde Hill' Ribbonwood, evergreen, white summer flowers

Juniperus scopulorum 'Skyrocket' Blue-grey juniper, spiny foliage makes ideal nest sites

Malus 'Van Eseltine' Narrow-growing crab apple, pink flowers in spring

Eucryphia lucida 'Pink Cloud' Letherwood evergreen with pink summer flowers, useful for bees

How can I make a garden wall more wildlife friendly?

IS A WALL JUST A BARRIER, or can it offer opportunities for wildlife and for gardeners? Do you have to grow climbers on walls to make them wildlife-friendly, or do bare bricks have any value for nature?

Garden walls can provide an incredibly varied habitat for all manner of wildlife. Bees, birds and even bats can appreciate their warmth and shelter. Plant them with climbers for maximum eco points, pick the right plants and your wall can become a high-performing habitat for wildlife.

A wall might sound like the ultimate 'unfriendly' garden feature. In fact, walls can offer a surprising number of habitats. Even bare walls may be home to the red mason bee (*Osmia bicornis*), a fuzzy little ginger bee that loves to nest in old nail-holes. Red mason bees are excellent pollinators, particularly of apple trees. If you have a sunny wall, but no old nail holes, try drilling some small holes and you may well find these lovely little creatures moving in.

East- or north-facing bare walls are also a great place to put bird boxes. Standard bird boxes for blue tits, starlings and sparrows should be positioned between 2–4m (6 and 12 ft) off the ground. If you have a really tall wall (more than 4m/14 ft) bat boxes are an option too.

For the very best wildlife value, plant a climber. Climbers can provide berries and natural nesting sites for birds, flowers for pollinating insects and habitat for all manner of garden creatures large and small. Plant climbers around 30cm (1 ft) or more away from the bottom of the wall. For support, attach wires threaded through vine eyes; or use trellis fixed to 6cm (2 in) battens screwed into the wall.

The cling-ons or self-fixing climbers

While most climbers will need some form of support to stay on the wall, a select group form their own attachment. Ivies, Virginia creeper, climbing hydrangea and trumpet vine (*Campsis*) all stick themselves to brickwork using specially modified (adventitious) roots or suckers. They don't damage sound brickwork.

Ivy
Hedera helix

WILDLIFE-FRIENDLY WALL PLANTS FOR SUN AND SHADE

Climbing hydrangea (shade), (*Hydrangea anomala* subsp. *petiolaris*) Pretty white flowers in summer, loved by bees. Thrives in shady gardens, tolerates some sun but won't enjoy a hot, dry spot. The leaves turn brilliant yellow before falling in autumn.

Climbing hydrangea (*Pileostegia viburnoides*) (shade) A hydrangea relative that bears fluffy white flowers in late summer and early autumn. Bees go mad for it. Needs shelter, shade and reliably moist soil. Evergreen, so will provide a winter refuge for some species.

Ivy (sun or shade), (*Hedera helix)* and cultivars. Ivy is a star wildlife plant, its dense evergreen growth shelters many animals through winter and its autumn flowers are a valuable source of nectar for pollinators. Birds enjoy its bluish black berries in winter and spring. There are lots of varieties available, including some with golden or variegated leaves.

Orange-peel clematis (sun or part shade), (*Clematis tangutica 'Bill Mackenzie'*) A lovely, multi-season, multi-purpose clematis. Bright orange-yellow flowers in late summer and autumn (a useful flowering time for bees) are followed by attractive, fluffy seedheads that make good nesting material for birds.

Firethorn (sun or part shade), (*Pyracantha*) Birds love pyracantha because its thorny branches give them safe nesting spots and its dramatic displays of red, orange or yellow berries are a useful food source too. Pollinating insects will appreciate its white flowers in late spring and early summer. Not a climber but easily trained against a wall.

Q Can eco-friendly gardening be economical?

Is ECO-FRIENDLY GARDENING just the preserve of people who can afford to buy a hybrid car and have space for a wildflower meadow? Does 'green' really just mean 'expensive' or are there ways to save cash while you're saving the planet?

Redcurrant
Ribes rubrum

B rush past the boutique bee hotels and hurry by the £50 hedgehog houses. Eco-friendly gardening is, at its core, about buying *less*, not more. Being truly 'green' means minimising external inputs (bought-in fertiliser, and so on), and prioritising homemade, recycled and repurposed items and DIY processes. So eco-friendly gardening is inherently economical.

Grow a money bush

Growing your own fruit and veg is very eco-friendly and, depending what you grow and how you grow it, pretty kind to your bank balance too. Easy, hardy crops have the best impact in this respect. Take a redcurrant bush, for example. The plant itself will cost you roughly £10 and will provide a crop for around ten years, easily giving you 3.5kgs (8 lbs) of fruit in a season. At current supermarket prices that's at least £525 worth of fruit and more than 200 plastic punnets saved. Plus the carbon footprint of transport and supermarkets. Not a bad return on investment.

A Eco-friendly gardening is by its very nature economical. At its core is the principle of buying less, not more. By adopting greener ways of gardening – such as growing plants from seed, making your own fertilisers and growing your own fruit and veg – you'll save cash while you're helping the environment.

ARE ALL FLOWERS EQUAL?

When it comes to flowers, not all are created equal. Growing your own flowers from seed sown straight into the earth is about as green and economical as you can get. But of course it's not always like that. Think of that perfect plant on a market stall or garden centre, lush, covered in flowers and utterly blemish-free. No information on where it was grown or who grew it. A foxglove in full flower in late March, rather than its usual July – a harbinger of the season ahead. Should you buy it?

It may well represent an ecological disaster. The black plastic pot is likely to be virgin, un-recycled and non-recyclable plastic. The compost is possibly almost 100 per cent peat, its very presence spelling ecological doom for a fragile peatbog and something of a climate crime for its carbon cost. The reason it looks so perfect is that it may well have been laced with insecticides, seed inhibitors and fungicides, some of which are so toxic that if bees feed on pollen from pesticide-treated plants, it impairs their offspring's brain development with 'permanent and irreversible' effects according to a recent study. And why is the foxglove in flower in March? Because it's grown in a heated greenhouse. This is an extreme example but it shows some of the true costs of buying in plants.

Be a savvy shopper

Wherever you can, buy smaller plants, buy bare-root and buy in season. Buy from local nurseries and ask for peat-free plants. Consider replacing bedding plants with perennials. Grow as many of your own plants as you can from seed. It's much, much cheaper. And much, much better for the world. Economical and ecological in equal measure.

Plastic not fantastic

Plastic is a sticking point as it's so cheap, and being waterproof it seems ideal for outdoor use. However, most plastic items degrade relatively rapidly in the high UV levels outdoors: netting weakens, watering cans crack, labels snap. So consider alternatives such as metal watering cans: they'll have infinitely longer lifespans so will save you money in the long run, and are repairable and recyclable so score green points too.

Does a wildlife garden have to be messy?

DOES A GARDEN need to be 'designed' to be successful, or can you just let it evolve over time? Are hard structures like paving essential, or are there alternatives?

Having a bit of mental structure – knowing what each part of the garden is for – is a good exercise for keeping your plans on track. Permaculture principles can be a useful guiding tool to help make your garden as wildlife and environmentally friendly as it can be, while providing useful things for humans too.

Working out a plan for your garden is a really useful way to get the most out of it. A plan can be anything from a detailed scale drawing on paper to a simple concept of what each area is for in terms of people and wildlife. Drawing out a plan can really help you make something beautiful and useful when designing a new garden; whereas in established gardens the groundwork might already be in place and you can work on developing concepts and differentiating areas. Keeping a garden diary is a helpful tool for planning. Having records to hand means you can trace what worked and

what didn't over the years and use that info to inform future choices.

'Structure' normally refers to the more solid parts of the design such as paths, hedges and fences. As a general rule, the softer and more natural the 'structure', the better it is for wildlife and the environment. For example, paths made of chipped bark or hoggin (a sandy clay-like material) have a much lower environmental impact than concrete or imported stone, and hedges have much better eco-credentials than fences or walls.

Can you have a neat garden and still encourage wildlife?

The best thing you can do for wildlife is to grow lots of plants, and put in a pond if you can. While some species undoubtedly appreciate undisturbed scruffiness, having a tidy garden doesn't mean there won't be any wildlife. One very famous wildlife garden surrounds a suburban semi-detached house in Leicester. Here, scientist Jennifer Owen recorded an incredible 2,673 species of plants and animals in her 'neat, productive plot' during a 30-year study.

LESSONS FROM PERMACULTURE

Permaculture is an eco-friendly way of gardening and living that is designed to meet human needs while enhancing biodiversity. It offers many handy ways of thinking about your space. Permaculture also stresses minimum work for maximum reward, and takes a more holistic approach to 'reward' – which might not be produce or cash, but health and wellbeing benefits. Here are a selection of permaculture principles that are particularly relevant to home gardens:

Observe and interact Get to know your garden and its resident wildlife before picking up a spade. Issues like shade from trees, space for parking cars or preventing local flooding can all be more easily resolved by getting to know your neighbours and collaborating with them.

Obtain a yield Yield can be delicious homegrown fruit and veg, or it can be wellbeing benefits. Think about the different yields each element of your garden can bring.

Produce no waste Recycle through composting, think about where the products you buy come from and how you can dispose of them and their packaging when you're finished with them.

Design from patterns to details Look at the big picture of what your garden is trying to achieve, what its underlying conditions are and design from those, rather than trying to impose something where it's not suitable.

Garden ponds are hugely valuable for wildlife and can be very beautiful too.

Are all hedges good for wildlife?

PLANTING A HEDGE to replace a fence is a win for nature. But are all hedging plants equal when it comes to wildlife value and other environmental benefits? And what situations are they suitable for?

Western red cedar
Thuja plicata

Yew
Taxus baccata

Hedges are great for the environment on many levels. Providing food and shelter for wildlife is an obvious benefit, but they have many more subtle effects. They reduce air and noise pollution, slow down rainwater run-off which helps prevent flooding, and sequester carbon from the atmosphere. Seeing a green hedge rather than a wall or fence has wellbeing benefits for people too.

Once established, hedges are also wind-proof. So by planting one you'll not only do your bit for nature but you'll also escape any ongoing costs of having to replace fence panels after storms. Remember that different plants are suitable for different heights of hedging, so it's worth doing a bit of research first. Select the right species to avoid either having to cut your hedge continually or having a very long wait to get it to your desired height. Always check that a fence is actually yours rather than your neighbour's before replacing it.

Pollution-busting

In front gardens facing busy roads, each hedging plant can capture as much as 60 diesel cars' worth of pollution a year! Yew (*Taxus baccata*), cotoneasters and western red cedar (*Thuja plicata*) are all particularly valuable in this respect. Let your hedge grow to at least 1.5m (5 ft) high and 1m (3 ft) thick for maximum benefit.

Replacing a fence with a hedge is a fantastic move for wildlife and the environment. Hedges perform lots of ecosystem services, such as reducing pollution, preventing flooding and providing habitats for nesting birds. There are lots of different hedging plants available, so do some research to pick the right one for you.

FIVE HEDGES WITH ENVIRONMENTAL BENEFITS

Beech, (*Fagus sylvatica*) A native plant, beech is great for supporting wildlife and sequestering carbon. Its copper-coloured autumn leaves stay on the plant over winter. Suitable for hedges 1.2m (4 ft) to 6m (20 ft) high.

Rugosa (or beach) rose, (*Rosa rugosa*) An easy-to-grow rose with beautiful, fragrant pink or white flowers. Useful for pollinating insects and birds. Grows particularly well on sandy soils and by the sea. Suitable for hedges 1.2m (4 ft) to 1.5m (6 ft) high.

Privet, (*Ligustrum ovalifolium*) A classic suburban hedge plant for good reason. Pollution tolerant, it's also wildlife-friendly and will help prevent flooding too. Semi-evergreen so will keep most of its leaves in mild winters. Suitable for hedges 1.2m (4 ft) to 3m (10 ft) high.

Holly, (*Ilex aquifolium*) A much-loved native plant that's great for wildlife. Its prickly evergreen leaves and red berries make it an ideal bird habitat. Useful for noise reduction, it will grow well in shady spots too. Suitable for hedges 1.2m (4 ft) to 5m (16 ft) high.

Western red cedar, (*Thuja plicata*) A better choice than Leylandii (*Cuprocyparis leylandii*) for most situations as it's not quite as rampant and grows back better when pruned hard. Recommended for noise reduction. Suitable for hedges 1.2m (4 ft) to 3m (10 ft) high.

Supporting wildlife

Prickly, flowering hedge plants such as pyracantha and hawthorn are especially valuable for wildlife. They provide shelter for birds and the thorns deter cats and other predators – birds don't seem to mind the spikes. They provide food for wildlife in the form of nectar and pollen from flowers, and berries for birds.

Privet
Ligustrum ovalifolium

Q Does compost have to come in plastic?

**IF YOU'RE TRYING TO CUT DOWN PLASTIC
use, compost can be a tricky area. Does it
always have to come in plastic bags? Are the
bags re-usable? Are there alternatives to
buying compost in new plastic bags?**

A Some garden centres now sell compost in re-usable 'bags for life', and the only way to expand schemes like these is through continued consumer pressure. Alternatively, bulk-buying reduces plastic waste, and compost bags can be re-used. Stable yards and council composting schemes can be good sources of material to bag up yourself.

A nyone who's been gardening for a while will have one. A pile of used compost bags, a folded up bag library or just a bag full of other bags. It can be frustrating that such a 'green' activity as gardening seems to create so much plastic pollution.

Plastic bags are a problem because they take centuries to degrade, devastating the environment as they do (around a third of all plastic packaging produced ends up in the ocean). Even if they can be recycled, they often aren't. It's best to avoid them as much as possible, and re-use those that you have. Bags for compost, bark, sand and gravel can all easily be re-used.

A great way to re-use old bags is to fill them with manure from local stables. Well-rotted farmyard manure is good for soil structure and fertility, and generally stable owners are delighted to get rid of it.

PLASTIC-FREE WAYS TO IMPROVE YOUR SOIL

Grow a green manure (see pp. 55), this is one of the most eco-friendly ways to improve your soil. Bulk-buy if you can; this is a great idea for allotments or if you're buying soil improver for a new garden. You'll save lots of cash along with plastic!

Where should I start with a new garden?

NATURE IS CAPRICIOUS, and gardens can be full of surprises. Sometimes the most lovingly placed plant will fail, and the one you thought you gave up on miraculously will burst into bloom. How can you increase your chances of success?

A bit of trial and error is inevitable in any garden. Get to know your site and soil conditions by spending time in your garden and observing it closely over time, the better you know your garden the more successful you will have.

Get to know your garden

Observe where the windy spots are, where the frost lingers and where the sun is at different times of day; a wall that catches the morning sun could be plunged into shade by midday.

Do this over a few months to really get a feel for the space. You might discover a corner that always stays wet for a few days after it's rained, the perfect place for a moisture-loving plant like Siberian iris (*Iris sibirica*).

Look at the weeds too. Sometimes the wild relatives of our garden plants will arrive of their own accord and give a helping hint from mother nature.

Herb robert (*Geranium robertianum*) is a cousin of our hardy cranesbills, so if you see it, why not plant one, such as the delightful *Geranium* 'Orion'?

What weeds can tell you about your soil

The plants that have managed to install themselves and thrive without any help are in some ways helpful allies to the gardener, as they give a good indication of the soil and general conditions.

Nettles (*Urtica dioica*) are gross feeders and are only found in abundance where the soil is rich and fertile. Cut them back before they seed and add them to the compost heap or use to make a liquid fertiliser.

Dandelions (*Taraxacum* spp.) are adapted to grow in compacted soils. Their sturdy taproots are able to break through where others can't, giving them a competitive advantage. This is a really good thing for long-term soil health as they bring up nutrients to the surface, helping other plants to establish themselves.

Will terracing work in an eco-garden?

TERRACING IS USED in many places across the world to allow farming on even the steepest slopes. Think of terraced olive groves on Mediterranean hillsides or stepped rice paddies in Southeast Asia. But is this technique suitable for gardens in the UK?

If you live on a slope, terracing can be a great way to get more usable space. Where gardens rise up away from the house, creating a generously sized terrace at the same level as the house will transform the way you feel about your garden.

The basic principle is to use a series of walls running across a slope. Each wall holds back a proportion of the slope, which is then levelled out between the top of one wall and the bottom of the next. If your slope isn't too steep, only one or two terrace walls will be necessary.

Terracing is hard work, but the rewards are great. It is a useful way to get much more usable space out of a sloping garden. Why not use the different terraces to make themed areas such as a wildflower meadow or vegetable patch? The terrace walls themselves can be attractive features in their own right.

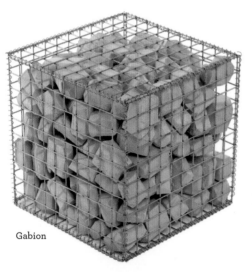

Gabion

Getting creative with gabion filling. Old machinery parts, rock, slate, airbricks, broken pots or pieces of pipe will make interesting fillings.

Broken pots

Old machinery

Logs

 You can use a range of different materials to fill gabions. Some, such as airbricks and logs can become useful wildlife habitats in their own right.

Reclaimed structural bricks

Gabions to the rescue

Generally terracing is an expert job, best left to professionals. However on shallow slopes you may be able to do it yourself. Gabions (metal baskets filled with rocks) make excellent retaining walls and are a useful DIY option.

Gabions come as flat-packed panels which are attached by inserting coiled corkscrew pins into the corners. Once the bottom and sides are fixed in place they can then be filled with rocks, large pebbles or other heavy materials – try to use local stone if you can. Gabions avoid the need for complex building work as they are held in place by their own weight. Just be sure to attach each gabion to its neighbour before filling them.

To save money you can fill the back half of your gabions with rubble, and only use decorative stone in the front half, which is the only part you'll see once the soil is filled in behind them. This is especially useful in new-build gardens where there may be a lot of rubble to get rid of.

Where there isn't a great weight of soil to be held back, you can consider lighter fillings for gabions. Logs or thick branches cut to the same length can make a wildlife-friendly filling, or try using airbricks, sections of clay pipe or old tiles stacked in attractive patterns.

ECO-TERRACES

If your garden is going to have a number of different terraces, try giving each one a distinctive theme. For example, in a sunny garden you could have a wildflower meadow terrace above a vegetable garden terrace. When you're doing the groundwork, move as much topsoil down as you can from the wildflower terrace onto the veg patch terrace. Your wildflower meadow needs thin, poor soil to let the flowers thrive among the grasses, and your veg will flourish in the deeper soil below.

Chapter 3

Greener Edibles

Are any vegetables pest-proof?

IF YOU'VE EVER GROWN CABBAGES it can feel like every pest in the neighbourhood knows about it. This can be hard to deal with if want perfect-looking leaves and don't enjoy having a garden full of netting or reaching for a spray. Are there any vegetables that pests don't seem to bother with?

Some vegetables are naturally less prone to attack by garden pests, such as courgettes, beans and chard. Plants in the cabbage family, especially those that take a long time to grow, such as cauliflowers, are much more at risk. Getting to know your enemy and changing your growing practices to grow out of sync with pest life cycles can help too.

Large white
butterfly
Pieris brassicae

Cabbage
Brassica

In a way, you could think of cabbages as the ultimate wildlife-friendly vegetable. Dozens of other animals such as birds, large white (popularly known as cabbage whites) butterflies and whitefly want to share them with you. However, all these bugs and gastropods are just another part of the food chain.

If most of your crop gets eaten, you could try covering your cabbages with extremely fine netting, growing companion crops and encouraging predators... or you could just grow something else.

Outwitting the pests

You can make some vegetables much more pest-proof by changing your sowing times. Carrot fly is a horrid little pest whose maggots hollow out carrot roots, making them inedible. However, if you sow your carrots after mid-May your crops should avoid the first generation of the fly. Harvest before late August and you'll avoid the second. If flea beetles disfigure your rocket crops every summer, try growing it in your greenhouse over winter, it can be sown in early autumn.

Slug
Gastropoda

Growing crops of mini veg is another way to out-fox the pests. Grow baby carrots, kale and broccoli during the warm, long days of late spring and summer. By sowing at this time and harvesting while still small you'll be keeping growing time (and hence exposure to pests) to a minimum.

All these crops can be susceptible to attack but by growing this way you're more likely to get to them before the pests discover them.

BUZZ OFF! PEST-PROOF VEGETABLES

• Perpetual spinach (also known as spinach beet) is a really useful crop that avoids almost all the pests commonly attack other leafy vegetables, most of which are in the brassica or cabbage family. Even pigeons tend to leave it alone.

• Beans – while peas may be munched by mice as soon as you sow them, and pigeons as soon as they have leaves, all kinds of beans are generally much more pest-proof. Runner and French beans are particularly good in this regard.

• Courgettes are generally trouble-free and massively productive. The only time they're really in any danger is when they're small plants as they can be vulnerable to slugs and snails. Once they're above about 20cm (8 in) tall you're in the clear.

• Pumpkins and squashes are closely related to courgettes and are just as pest-free. Protect young plants from slugs, and enjoy watching their rampant growth. Great to grow with children – if you want a giant pumpkin only allow one fruit per plant.

• Rhubarb, although often considered a fruit, is actually a vegetable, and a very pest-resistant one at that. Its tart flavour works brilliantly in savoury dishes – counterbalancing the richness of mackerel or pork, or in Asian-style sweet and sour dishes.

Rhubarb
Rheum rhabarbarum

What are the secrets of growing from seed?

SOWING SEEDS, watching them germinate and then grow into beautiful plants is one of the most profound pleasures of gardening. Is there a standard technique that works for all seeds? Do you have to follow the instructions on the packet to the letter?

Seed sowing 101

A simple rule for seed sowing is to cover the seed with its own depth with compost or soil. So the smaller the seed, the more shallowly it should be sown, and vice versa. Big seeds like peas and beans will be fine in multipurpose compost. If seeds are tiny, sow them on the surface of a specialist seed compost and cover them with either a fine layer of vermiculite or a plastic cover (ideally both). Always use peat-free compost.

Read the packet!

Instructions on packets give you the ideal conditions for seeds to germinate. Use them as a guide; even if you don't follow them exactly you'll probably still have some success.

Seed sowing isn't an exact science and you'll always have surprises. Use the packet instructions as a guide but don't worry too much if you can't follow them precisely. The only thing that's certain is that if you leave them in the packet, they definitely won't grow!

Sowing times are generally more important than precise temperatures. For example, tomatoes need to be sown early so they can make big plants in

▼ Growing plants from seed is hugely rewarding – it never loses its thrill no matter how many times you do it!

1. Cover seeds with their own depth of compost or soil

2. Follow instructions for the best light conditions and temperature

3. Plant outside once the chance of frost has passed.

ARE SOME SEEDS GREENER THAN OTHERS?

There are a few words for the eco-gardener to look out for on seed packets. 'Treated seed' can be coated in a chemical such as a fungicide, which will have an effect on your garden's wildlife on some level. Read the packet carefully to see what the treatment is. F1 hybrids are artificial crosses between two selections of the same plant – their production is less environmentally friendly than that of normal (open-pollinated) seed, and you can't save seed yourself for next year, although F1 vegetable crops do tend to yield more than other varieties.

The greenest seeds of all are those you've saved yourself. Runner beans, poppies and French marigolds are all easy to grow from self-saved seeds. Beware that some plants, such as white foxgloves and squashes, as well as any F1 hybrid plants you have in your garden, won't come true from seed.

The best place to store your seeds is in a sealed plastic container in the fridge or cupboard. Darkness and cool even temperatures are key. Don't keep them in a greenhouse or shed as this could shorten their life considerably.

time for midsummer and give you lots of crops, whereas if you sow dwarf French beans early they'll peak too soon and miss the summer heat they need to give their best.

Some seeds need light, some need dark in which to germinate – this will also determine the sowing depth. Depending on the plant, they may need warmth (such as French beans) or cold periods (such as many hardy trees like oaks and beeches) to germinate.

Use your judgement when it comes to sowing outdoors; particularly in early spring. If the soil is too cold, your seeds won't germinate. When sowing

Field poppy
*Papaver
rhoeas*

hardy crops like beetroot and carrots, check if weed seedlings have started to appear. If they're beginning to grow you'll know the soil is warm enough to sow your crops.

'Sow-by' dates are more useful on some plants than others. You'll struggle to grow carrots and parsnips from packets more than a year out of date. Peas, broad beans and poppies may well surprise you.

Q How can I produce more compost?

HOMEMADE COMPOST is rocket fuel for healthy happy gardens. Sweet-smelling, crumbly and brown, it brings soil to life and makes plants grow bigger and better. Almost all plants will benefit from it – the more compost you can make the better. So how do you make more of this wonderful stuff?

A Get thinking about those greens and browns – suddenly there can be more sources of composting material than you ever realised. Getting them moist and mixing them together is key to successful composting. Once you've produced a successful batch, composting can be surprisingly addictive!

Brown

Woody prunings

Green

Grass clippings

Green

Kitchen scraps

A lmost any garden waste will rot down eventually and enrich the soil in some way. The key to making good compost quickly is getting a mix of drier, woodier ingredients with damper, greener ingredients.

The woody materials are generally referred to as 'browns', and include woody prunings, cardboard and any straw-like dead stems. They are carbon-rich, giving body and structure to the compost. 'Greens', such as

A dynamic mix of both household and garden waste can contribute to a healthy compost heap.

lawn clippings and kitchen scraps, are damper and give nutrients (particularly nitrogen) to the mix. This is why some books refer to the carbon:nitrogen ratio when making compost.

Think of compost like making a pasta dish. You want there to be a good ratio of pasta (browns) to sauce and other ingredients (greens). Mix it all in well. Keep it moist but not wet, tread it down lightly so everything is in contact but not compacted and airless. Balancing these different elements – carbon, nitrogen, air and water – is key to making great compost.

Making more compost

Shredders are invaluable tools for making more compost more quickly. By shredding your prunings from trees and shrubs you maximise their surface area, making them much more digestible by the hidden army of fungi, bacteria and invertebrates that turn waste into brown gold.

If you're shredding lots of brown woody material, be sure to mix in plenty of greens, such as veg peelings or lawn clippings. If you don't have enough green material to fully balance out the brown, consider using it as a mulch in the garden. Or water it well as you add it, and sprinkle over some nitrogen-rich additives like compost activators or pelleted chicken manure which will help it break down.

A decent shredder can be expensive. However, you don't have to own one – club together with neighbours or hire one as you need it. That way you'll save cash and garage space, as well as the environmental impact of manufacturing fewer items.

Lawnmowers are the compost heap's friend. Lawn clippings are the most abundant source of 'greens' for the heap. If you leave fallen leaves on the lawn in autumn and mow them up along with the grass you'll have the ideal starting point for great compost, because what you collect will be the perfect mix of 'greens' and 'browns'.

COMPOSTING DOS AND DON'TS

Unexpected things you can compost

- Pure wool jumpers
- Vaccuumings from the house
- Dog or cat fur, human hair
- Cotton clothes (only if 100 per cent cotton)
- Soiled hamster/gerbil/ rabbit bedding

What shouldn't I compost?

- Poo (except from herbivores such as rabbits)
- Meat and dairy waste
- Many 'compostable' plastics such as disposable glasses will take a long time to break down in domestic compost heaps

Which vegetables are most energy efficient to grow?

GROWING YOUR OWN VEG ranks pretty highly in the scale of green activities. You can eliminate almost all energy costs compared to supermarket vegetables – homegrown wins in terms of transport but also represents big savings in energy use from processing, storing and packaging too. But which crops are the most energy efficient of all?

The energy efficiency of homegrown crops depends on what you grow and how you grow it.

Hardy crops such as beetroot, carrots and broad beans are the least energy intensive of all. This is because they are sown directly into the soil, outdoors. By sowing directly you sidestep the potential energy costs associated with growing under cover. No plastic pots, no carbon footprint of manufacturing and transporting compost and no heated propagators needed.

It's all in the timing

Many crops can be sown earlier under cover. This is useful in cooler northern climates but isn't critical in warmer gardens. Sweetcorn, runner beans, French beans, courgettes and pumpkins are all examples of plants that can be sown outdoors quite happily once the risk of frost has passed.

Pumpkins can be sown direct outdoors in late May, saving on pots and compost.

The most energy-efficient crops are those that you can sow directly into the ground rather than those that need sowing in pots indoors. So if you're concerned about energy efficiency, try carrots, beetroot, broad beans and other hardy crops. Perennial vegetables are worth considering too as they're even lower input. Grow green manures (see p. 55) to improve your soil's fertility without the need to use energy-intensive fertilisers.

ENERGY-EFFICIENT VEG

Go for veg that don't need replanting every year. Although they're generally not quite as productive as annual crops they're a lot less work. Here are five of the best:

Asparagus: A very long-lived crop – asparagus beds can be productive for well over a decade, so they make a great return on investment.

Welsh onions: These are like a clump of chunky spring onions, with greenish-white pompom flowers. Pick the stems as you need them and use as you would spring onions.

Globe artichokes: Tall, handsome plants that grow easily in sunny sites. Sow a few extra so the bees can enjoy their thistle-like flowers.

Perpetual spinach (also called spinach beet): Will crop for months on end, providing tasty nutritious leaves and stems. Useful as steamed greens or in pasta. Not a true perennial but much longer-lasting than standard spinach.

Jerusalem artichokes: These sunflower-like plants produce knobbly tubers in autumn.

Chilli
Capsicum annuum

Going under cover

Some crops such as chillies and aubergines do absolutely need to be sown under cover in heated conditions, so demand more energy. Grafted vegetable plants are generally considered to be more productive than seed-raised ones – however it's unclear whether this increase in yield would outweigh their more energy-intensive production methods and their transport costs.

Greenhouses and polytunnels require energy to make; however that is more than compensated for by the increased productivity you get from the crops growing inside. Second-hand aluminium greenhouses are a good bet as they last almost indefinitely, and every part can be recycled too.

High-energy gardening

Artificial chemical fertilisers take a lot of energy to make; they account for 1 per cent of all global emissions of greenhouse gases. Opt for organic and homemade fertilisers such as pelleted chicken manure or comfrey tea instead. Nitrogen-fixing green manures are a great way to enrich your soil in an energy-efficient way. Try clover, field beans and common vetch.

Is growing from seed greener than buying small plants in?

SOWING SEEDS AND WATCHING your babies germinate and flourish is hugely satisfying. But is it worth it when you can save time and effort buying small plants from the garden centre?

Cucumber
Cucumis sativus

By growing your own plants from seed, you can be sure exactly how 'green' your plants really are. Unless the plants you buy in are labelled as organic or peat free, they will probably have been grown using chemicals and peat – both of which are bad for the environment. Growing from seed also gives you the maximum choice when it comes to varieties.

Plastic is a burning issue; while it's hard for home gardeners to avoid, you can at least re-use it a number of times, saving on the virgin plastic that comes with bought-in plants. Peat is another sticking point. Most plants for sale are still grown in peat-based composts, although some companies are starting to offer peat-free options. Also, particularly for edible crops like tomatoes, you'll have a far greater choice of varieties available as seed rather than plants.

There are a number of ways in which growing your own from seed can beat buying plants in. Unless your plants are labelled 'organic', they will most likely have been sprayed with chemicals such as fungicides and pesticides. Some pesticides used in ornamental horticultural production have been linked to damaging the nervous systems of bees – weeks or even months after they were applied to the plant.

EXCEPTIONS TO THE RULE

Sometimes it's worth buying in a small plant or two if you need a head start. For example, with chillies, you only need one or two plants, plus they need lots of heat and light and a long season to get them going.

Can I protect my fruit trees?

EATING FRESH off the tree is one of the great pleasures of gardening. Unfortunately humans aren't alone in appreciating a juicy cherry or crisp apple. Birds, bugs and other creatures all want to get in on the action. What can gardeners do to make sure their trees stay healthy and their harvests make it into the kitchen rather than go straight on the compost heap?

There are lots of ways to protect your fruit trees and get good harvests. Physical methods such as netting keeps out birds and training fruit trees against a wall or fence makes them much easier to protect. Rather than reaching for the spray gun at the first sign of a caterpillar it's best to accept sharing some of the harvest with the wildlife that shares your garden.

Cherry blossom
Prunus sp.

GET TRAINING!

The easiest way to protect fruit trees from marauding birds is to grow your fruit trees trained as espaliers or fans against a wall or fence. This not only looks great but it also makes it much easier to attach nets over the trees.

Birds can be a big problem for fruit growers. They love cherries in particular, but almost any fruit tree is susceptible to attack. The best solution is to net your trees, if you can. Not all netting is equal though; cheap plastic netting is rarely a bargain as it tears and tangles easily and some types degrade quickly in sunlight. Choose higher specification grades – they'll more than make up for their higher cost by having a much longer life-span.

In rural areas, it's advisable to use trunk guards to protect against rabbit damage. Rabbits can really damage younger trees with more tender bark. Use spiral rabbit guards (there are biodegradable versions available) or chicken wire – but be sure to loosen it as the tree grows.

Can I get a harvest from pots?

GROWING CROPS IN POTS is a useful way to maximise your growing space, and it also allows you to grow fruit and veg that aren't suitable for your soil type. But are all crops suited to container growing? Which should you choose for worthwhile harvests?

There are a number of good reasons to grow crops in pots and containers. First, they allow you to grow almost anywhere – from windowsills to tiny balconies and patios, pots make it possible. Second, they allow you to create the ideal soil conditions for your favourite crops. For example, if you love blueberries but you don't have the acidic soil conditions they need, grow them in pots of acidic (ericaceous) compost. Carrots need soil without too many stones in it; if yours is full of flint then try growing them in deep pots of sandy compost and you'll be amazed at the difference.

Very vigorous, tall leafy crops such as runner beans will dry out quickly in containers and be vulnerable to

Growing fruit and veg in pots is easy, fun and extremely satisfying. Blueberries, strawberries and salads in particular will all give you delicious crops for not too much effort. Dwarf varieties of fruits and vegetables are generally the most suitable for container growing as they're simpler to look after – they're easier to keep watered and less likely to blow over in high winds.

Champion carrot growers cultivate their crops in enormous containers of sandy compost.

POTTED PLEASURES – STAR PERFORMERS FOR CONTAINER GROWING

• Potatoes – if you love the taste of new potatoes but hate digging, try growing them in containers. Many retailers sell special 'potato sacks' or planters, although there are potential sustainability issues with these. Use homemade compost if you have it.

• Blueberries are perhaps the ultimate container crop. They produce abundant fruit in late summer, and they also give attractive autumn colour and pretty spring flowers. Use peat-free ericaceous compost. Select a self-fertile variety or, ideally, grow a couple of varieties.

• Strawberries grow well in containers, you can even try them in window boxes. Some varieties have attractive pink flowers. Look

for 'everbearing' varieties for a long season crop. Miniature alpine varieties look especially cute. Use peat-free multipurpose compost.

• Carrots can be difficult to grow well in open ground if your soil is stony. Sow seeds in a tall container of sandy compost and you'll get beautiful straight roots. Or try round-rooted varieties if you don't have deep pots.

• Salads are useful in small spaces: grow cut-and-come-again varieties, and loose-leaf rather than hearting lettuce. That way you can just pick what you need. Old grow-bags are ideal for salad crops. Grow a range of shapes and colours, such as frilly purple mustard leaves, red lettuce and mizuna, for pots that taste as good as they look.

blowing over in high winds. Choose smaller varieties, such as 'Hestia', which is naturally dwarf. Fruit trees can be grown in large pots – look for patio ranges of crops, such as peaches and apricots. These are grown on special rootstocks to reduce their vigour, making them much more suitable for container cultivation.

Which pots are best?
Earthy-coloured terracotta pots have a timeless beauty but beware! They are porous, so will lose water extremely quickly. This makes it quite a battle to keep your plants happy. One dry, breezy summer day and your plants will dry out completely within hours. So stick to shiny glazed pots or use recycled plastic and metal containers.

Are distraction crops effective?

IF MARIGOLDS are planted near tomatoes, do the whitefly go to the marigolds and not the crops? What other ways can you distract pests from your edible crops?

The various companion planting techniques have little hard evidence to support them, but a wealth of anecdotal evidence. There's no harm in giving distraction crops a try!

What is companion planting?

Communities of plants are grown together for the benefit of each other and the whole garden. A healthy garden growing in harmony – working with nature rather than against it – reduces the need for petro-chemicals, weedkillers and pesticide sprays, and allows insects and other wildlife to flourish.

By utilising companion plants, the effects of pests can be significantly diminished.

By growing plants that are known to attract insect predators (such as hoverflies, lacewing flies and ladybirds), pests can be easily kept in check.

Growing different plants together can significantly reduce the threat of a pest or disease sweeping through a crop.

Some plants can be grown as a sacrifice to the pests, such as a border of lettuce to keep slugs at bay, and nasturtiums to attract aphids to them rather than beans and other veg.

Other companion plants exude chemicals either from their foliage or their roots that can help deter pests, diseases and even weeds, a phenomenon known as allelopathy.

▼ Growing plants such as marigolds in between veg crops can attract pest predators and/or deter pests with their strong fragrance.

WHAT OTHER WAYS CAN I GROW PLANTS TOGETHER?

The simplest way is to mix vegetables in with the rest of the garden rather than having a dedicated veg patch, such as having soft fruit bushes in a shrub border, or using a forest gardening technique. Growing plants for pollinators also helps ensure a good harvest (see pp. 122–3). The following plants all have a strong fragrance that is thought to deter pests – plant them in the veg patch and see what happens:

• Summer savory (*Satureja hortensis*)

• Tobacco plant (*Nicotiana taburnum*) especially to deter large white butterflies

• Garlic chives (*Allium tuberosum*)

• Basil (*Ocimum basilicum*) – can also be used as a sacrificial plant for whitefly infestations

• Mint (*Mentha* sp.)

• Wormwood (*Artemisia absinthium*)

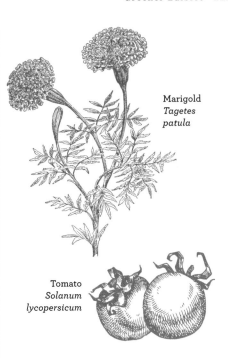

Marigold
Tagetes patula

Tomato
Solanum lycopersicum

Does the marigold/tomato combination work?

The strongly scented foliage of both *Tagetes patula* and *T. minima* – although not pot marigolds (*Calendula officinalis*) – deters aphids and whitefly, especially when grown in large numbers and/or in the confines of a greenhouse. Plus, the bright flowers attract hoverflies and ladybirds, which predate on aphids both as adults and as their odd-looking larvae, so they could offer some protection to the tomatoes if grown nearby. The roots of *Tagetes minuta* also exude sulphurous compounds known as thiopenes, which deter and inhibit the growth of eelworms (soil-borne pests) and slugs and are toxic to some perennial weeds.

Is it greener to grow native veg than to try exotics?

YOU'RE TRYING TO MAKE your garden as wildlife-friendly as possible, planting lots of native plants. Is trying to stick to native vegetables a logical step in the right direction? Are native vegetables easier to grow, since they evolved in our climate?

Parsnip
Pastinaca sativa

Which vegetables are native to Britain?

You might be surprised to learn that lots of vegetables we consider to be quintessentially British are actually anything but. Runner beans came over from Mexico and potatoes hail from Peru. Although peas have been grown in Britain for millennia, they're originally from the Mediterranean region.

If you want to grow a purely native veggie banquet you'll be pretty much limited to carrots, parsnips, cabbages and beets. These 'native' veg have been domesticated so much over the centuries that some of them bear hardly any resemblance to their wild cousins. Brussels sprouts are technically the same species as our wild cabbage, but you'd never find them growing wild on a windy clifftop on the south coast. So it could be argued they're no longer native at all.

A Don't bother trying to prioritise native veg – you'll quickly get bored of eating just a few crops. Even so-called 'native' crops tend to have been bred so much they're barely recognisable from the wild plant, so you could say they're no longer native. Grow what you like eating and enjoy it; you're already doing your bit for the planet!

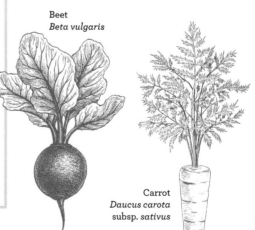

Beet
Beta vulgaris

Carrot
Daucus carota
subsp. *sativus*

Wren
*Troglodytes
troglodytes*

Go native for wildlife?

The wildlife angle is an interesting one. Certainly it could be argued that native veg are good for wildlife (see p. 70). Just look at all the species of insects and birds that will throw themselves at a row of unprotected cabbages.

While caterpillars are wildlife just as much as the blue tits that feast on them, do you really want to share your cabbages with them? Natives aren't any easier to grow – they might have evolved to suit our climate perfectly but they've also been around long enough for lots of wildlife (pests) to get a taste for them too. Non-native crops such as runner beans and sweetcorn often – though not always – tend to suffer from fewer pests.

Given that there are so many wildlife-friendly plants out there that don't happen to be vegetables, and the whole native question is potentially up for debate anyway (see p. 74), it's pretty safe to say you don't need to worry about whether your vegetables are native or not.

GOING WILD

To get a true taste of native vegetables, try foraging. Some of the uncultivated edible plants that grow wild in the countryside are absolutely delicious, and free!

Nettles (*Urtica dioica*) are the star wild veg as they're abundant, nutritious and versatile. Pick the young growth in spring and use in soups, pesto and stuffed pasta. Wild garlic (*Allium ursinum*), ground elder (*Aegopodium podagraria*) and dandelions (*Taraxacum* spp.) are also useful.

A few necessary precautions: don't pick near busy roads, in nature reserves or SSSIs, and ask the landowner's permission if you're on private ground. Always be sure to thoroughly check the identity of anything you eat and never dig up the roots. The golden rule: if in doubt, chuck it out!

If you are still keen to cultivate native, wildlife-friendly edibles, grow fruit. Raspberries, blackberries and currants are all native and are all great for bees – and birds if you let them eat the fruit!

Is it still green to grow year-round crops?

TO MANY PEOPLE, growing your own is mostly about picking strawberries in July along with tomatoes and runner beans in August and September. But what about the rest of the year? Is it possible to enjoy homegrown harvests every single month?

With a bit of forward planning it is possible to pick something edible from your garden every day of the year, even from a modest-sized plot. The main tricks to doing this is to ensure you're growing some long-lasting crops and to make repeat sowings of other crops.

And repeat! Successional sowing

It's a common mistake made by new gardeners. You buy a packet of lettuce seed and sow it. All of it. And two months later you have more lettuce than you can possibly eat followed by nothing at all.

By sowing in small batches, over an extended period of time, you can prolong your harvests. This is called 'successional sowing' and it's key to breaking the feast or famine cycle.

Successional sowing is best suited to fast-growing crops like lettuces, spring onions and radishes. These are the 'live fast and die young' crew – if you wait too long to harvest them, they'll run to seed and become inedible. Sow every few weeks over the spring, summer and early autumn.

Other crops crops, such as carrots and beetroot, last longer in their prime but still benefit from a repeat sowing or two. For example, a sowing in March followed by one in May and another in July. Fruiting veg like tomatoes and cucumbers don't need succession sowing because each plant can produce a crop over a long period of time anyway.

Salad crops

▶ Choose modern, hardier varieties of tender crops such as melons, which won't need extra heating.

Don't force it!

Many older gardening books suggest heating greenhouses to get out of season crops. This made sense at a time when fuel was cheap, fewer people had freezers and no-one had heard of climate change. Today, gardeners have become more environmentally conscious, and fuel becomes ever more expensive. Not to mention the fact lots of garden produce can easily be frozen for winter – it's just not worthwhile for most of us to heat our greenhouses to grow food. Unheated greenhouses are still really useful for growing salads over winter, along with tender crops such as melons, tomatoes and sweet peppers in summer.

Mighty microgreens

If, like almost everyone else, you're not as organised as you'd like to be, then there are a few quick cheats to keep you in homegrown vegetables when you find yourself short. Microgreens are simply miniature salads and herbs grown in seed trays indoors and harvested when just a few centimetres high. Twenty-first century cress, basically! There are many available: fennel, radish, coriander and mizuna

THE HUNGRY GAP

The 'hungry gap' is a slightly old-fashioned term for the point in the year when your stored and winter crops have run out and your spring plantings are yet to provide a harvest. This occurs in April, May and sometimes into early June.

There are several ways to avoid the hungry gap. Grow spring greens (leafy cabbages sown in autumn), rhubarb and purple sprouting broccoli. If you have a greenhouse or polytunnel you can maximise its usefulness by sowing early salads, radishes, pea shoots, beetroot and baby carrots in February and March. And of course there's also asparagus...

are particularly tasty. Be sure to look for microgreen seed packets in seed catalogues as you'll get lots more seed for your money than in regular packets.

Can a polytunnel be eco-friendly?

IN A TIME WHEN 'PLASTIC-FREE' has become an environmental cause célèbre, is there still a place for polytunnels in our gardens and allotments? Do their eco-credentials outweigh their environmental costs, and can they be recycled?

The sheltered conditions polytunnels provide enable you to grow more variety of crops, more easily, in more parts of the country. They also give you bigger yields than crops grown outdoors and allow you to have year-round harvests. All this extra homegrown fruit and veg can seriously reduce the environmental impact of your diet.

By shielding plants from the worst of the weather, polytunnel growing can help reduce some diseases such as tomato and potato blight, and their warm conditions are ideal for using biological controls – all of which means less temptation for gardeners to use pesticides.

Re-using and recycling

Eventually, the polythene covering of your polytunnel will need to be replaced, either because the UV in sunlight has weakened it or because of rips or tears. But what to do with your old cover?

By helping you grow more crops over a longer period, polytunnels can really help reduce your diet's environmental impact. Look after your tunnel to get the maximum lifespan, and the eco-benefits of your crops should more than cover the environmental impact of its manufacture.

Re-use should always be first choice for the eco-minded gardener. However bad the damage, there will always be some usable bits left. These can be used to make cold frames, mini polytunnels to protect seedlings, or used as tarpaulins.

Covers are made from low-density polyethylene (LDPE), which is a recyclable material. However, it pays to check with your local authority first before adding it to the waste stream. LDPE is recycled to make garden refuse sacks, bin liners or silage wrap.

What is vegan gardening?

VEGANISM IS A GROWING MOVEMENT.
**How do vegan ethics translate to gardening?
Does vegan necessarily mean more
environmentally friendly?**

Growmore
fertiliser

According to The Vegan Society, veganism 'is a way of living which seeks to exclude, as far as is possible and practicable, all forms of exploitation of, and cruelty to, animals for food, clothing or any other purpose'.

You might be surprised at the amount of animal products involved in gardening, especially fertilisers and soil improvers – many of which are by-products of animal-based agriculture. If you're trying to be an eco-friendly gardener, it pays to be mindful when selecting products on the basis that they're technically vegan. It's not just a case of ditching the animal-based products, as many of the alternatives are synthetics based on fossil fuels.

Most advocates of vegan gardening take a much more holistic, organic approach, looking at ecosystems as a whole. So rather than switching from bonemeal (animal-based) to a synthetic vegan product, make your own compost and comfrey fertiliser. Your garden and its creatures – and the planet – will be all the happier for it.

Vegan gardening has, for many people, evolved into an organic, holistic approach which seeks to avoid potential harm to all creatures. There are lots of ways to do this, such as avoiding using animal-based manures and fertilisers by making plant-based ones at home; and using natural gardening techniques to minimise pest problems.

Creature-kind ways to garden

Use companion planting to help prevent pest problems, such as French marigolds next to tomatoes. Encourage natural predators such as hoverflies by planting pollinator-friendly flowers. Mulch, don't dig – digging disturbs the delicate ecosystem of the soil, and inevitably some creatures will be harmed in the process. So mulch with compost and let the worms pull it into the soil for you.

Q Are there more good insects than bad ones?

German wasp
Vespula germanica

THE VERY WORD 'INSECT' can conjure up some nasty associations – stinging wasps, annoying flies and scuttling cockroaches. But with more than 20,000 species of insect in Britain, are they all bad? Do the well-known villains such as wasps have some redeeming qualities too?

Common wasp
Vespula vulgaris

Our gardens are home to an incredible diversity of insects. In a ground-breaking 30-year study, scientist Dr Jennifer Owen studied the wildlife in her average-sized suburban garden in Leicester. She recorded nearly 2,000 insect species – although by her own admission some entire groups weren't counted, so the grand total could have been more like 8,500 according to ecologist and author Ken Thompson. That's in an area about twice the size of an IMAX screen (or one and a half basketball courts).

That astonishing total becomes even more amazing when you break it down. Dr Owen found 533 species of parasitic wasps. Big deal? Actually yes, when you consider that while they're harmless to humans, they're important predators of garden pests such as caterpillars and aphids. If you ever see hollow, papery-looking dead aphids on your plants, you'll know that these little allies have been hard at work.

Even the stingy, buzzing wasps we all know from summer picnics have their uses. Correctly – if somewhat ironically to non-scientists – known as 'social wasps' (perhaps it should be 'antisocial' wasps?), you're most likely to see the common wasp, (*Vespula vulgaris*) and the German wasp, (*Vespula germanica*) Both are important native pollinators and, like their parasitic cousins, love to feast on garden pests such as greenfly and caterpillars. The main difference is that they like to eat their prey by nibbling it from the outside in, rather than the parasites' habit of eating their way out. Isn't nature delightful sometimes?

A

Even modest-sized gardens can contain thousands of insect species, yet only a handful are classed as pests. Tolerating a few pests in your garden can help build up populations of their predators – aim for a balance and nature will lend you a generous helping hand.

TOP GARDEN INSECT ALLIES

Apart from wasps, there are a number of insect allies that do a great job helping gardeners with everything from pollinating crops to eating aphids.

Honeybee
Apis mellifera

Hoverflies (*Syrphiadae*) These harmless flies mimic wasps and bees for their own safety. The larvae of some species are voracious predators of aphids, and the adults help with pollination too. There are approximately 250 native species in the UK.

Hoverfly
Syrphidae

Ladybirds (*Coccinella* spp.) Peer closely at ladybird larvae: they're terrifying-looking, like sci-fi creatures with grey-black bodies covered in spikes and blobs of yellow and orange. Harmless to humans but each one can eat up to 5,000 aphids. There are between 26 and 43 species in the UK, depending on your definition.

Lacewings (*Chrysoperla carnea*) Another insect with pretty adults that come from ugly yet pest-hungry grubs. There are 18 species in the UK, most have shimmering green bodies, translucent wings and long antennae. Both adults and larvae enjoy eating aphids.

Bees (*Apis* spp.) There are a lot more bees than just honeybees. There are around 270 species in Britain; one of honeybee, 25 of bumblebees and the rest are called 'solitary bees'. They all pollinate flowers, which is important for crops like apples and raspberries.

Beetles (*Coleoptera*) Ground beetles and rove beetles are predators of all kinds of garden pests, from slugs and snails to red spider mites and aphids. There are around 1,300 beetle species in the UK.

Ladybird
Coccinella septempunctata

Lacewing
Chrysoperla carnea

Are traditional herb gardens eco-friendly?

SOME HERBS like ginger and ginseng have medicinal properties – do some of the herbs we grow have similar therapeutic qualities? What should you grow for herbal home remedies?

Yarrow
*Achillea
millefolium*

Many herbs have uses that extend far beyond the culinary, and most are also excellent at attracting pollinators and other beneficial insects. Make space for a herb patch of your own design, or use them to edge a veg or fruit patch.

Since the physic gardens of medieval monasteries, and indeed since Neanderthal man lived in Britain more than 40,000 years ago, humans have used herbs to heal and strengthen. Herbal medicine is still the *main* medicine for 80 per cent of the UN's member states. Herb garden design has changed through the ages from ordered lines of plants to teach the apothecarists in places like the Chelsea Physic Garden, to the knot gardens of the Elizabethans, to the billowing-yet-structured look of twentieth-century gardens such as Sissinghurst in Kent.

A healing cuppa

The therapeutic benefits of many herbs can be harnessed by making a simple herbal tea (also known as a tisane; technically they are hot-water infusions). Good herbs for teas to calm the digestion include mint, chamomile flowers and fennel seeds (crushed). To soothe and relax the mind during stressful times, try lemon balm, lavender or lime tree (*Tilia*) flowers. Lemon verbena doesn't appear to have any significant benefits, but it tastes delicious and makes a good addition to any tisane.

To make a herbal tea, take a handful of the fresh herbs – either a single herb or a mixture – and (having rinsed them first and/or checked for bugs,) tear them roughly and put into a teapot or cafetière. Otherwise put a lid over the mug; the aim is to prevent the herb oils escaping in the steam. Boil the kettle, leave it for a minute so the hot water doesn't scorch the leaves then pour over the herbs. Put the lid on and leave for up to 10 minutes before serving. Don't have a tisane of the same herbs more than three times a day.

Herbs for colds and flu

Other common garden herbs and garden plants are useful for helping our bodies recover from colds and flu. A cooled infusion of sage (made as above but allowed to cool completely before using) is an excellent gargle for a sore throat, and fresh eucalyptus leaves can be added to a basin of hot water for steam inhalation to clear nasal congestion. Raw garlic is proven to be a powerful support to the immune system.

Garden first aid

Many people are aware of the relief that a crushed plantain leaf (*Plantago major*) can bring to a nettle sting – it also works with chickweed (*Stellaria media*). Shallow scratches and cuts (washed in clean water to remove dirt) can be staunched with yarrow (*Achillea millefolium*), self-heal (*Prunella vulgaris*) and herb robert (*Geranium robertianum*) – and the leaves of the last rubbed on the skin will help to repel mosquitoes and other bugs.

> ### CAUTION WHEN USING HERBS FOR HOME REMEDIES
>
> Always be sure you have identified the plant correctly, use it in moderation and not for children under the age of two. Many herbs have contraindications during pregnancy and breastfeeding. Consult a qualified herbalist or medical professional if in any doubt.

▼ Herbs are particularly valuable plants for pollinating insects, as well as providing healing benefits for the gardener.

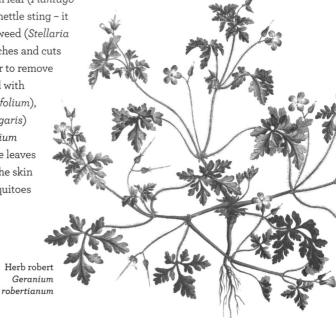

Herb robert
Geranium robertianum

How can I attract bees and other pollinators to my veg plot?

BEES AND OTHER POLLINATING INSECTS are surprisingly useful allies when it comes to growing your own veg. Not only will they pollinate crops, such as strawberries, that need fertilisation to produce a yield, some of these winged wonders can help reduce pest problems too. So how do you lure them in?

Who needs bees?

Bees and other pollinators are vital for successful harvests of almost all fruit-bearing crops. So this means all tree and soft fruit, obviously, but also courgettes, squashes, pumpkins and so on. Unpollinated, flowers on these plants fall off and die, and you get no harvest at all. Pollination is also vital if you want to save your own seeds.

Bring bees and other pollinators to your plot by including plenty of flowering plants alongside your vegetables. Many herbs are great for pollinating insects and useful in the kitchen, so planting a herb garden within or next to your veg plot is a handy way to benefit wildlife and your culinary creations at the same time.

Some pollinators are also predators – especially hoverflies and wasps (see pp. 118–19) so they'll help sort out pest problems too. Hoverfly larvae live on a diet of aphids while wasps are useful predators of caterpillars.

Bringing in the bees

A golden rule of pollinator-friendly gardening is to put down the spray gun. Insecticides can very easily kill or injure bees, butterflies and a host of garden allies. In particular, avoid spraying plants in flower, even with organic or homemade sprays. Encourage pollinators to linger longer by providing habitats such as insect hotels and bee drinkers – shallow trays of water and pebbles that allow insects to drink safely.

Make room for some flowers. Many herbs have beautiful, pollinator-friendly flowers and make useful accompaniments to homegrown fruit and veg. Grow some cut flowers, leaving some uncut for the pollinators, and allow a few veg plants to go to seed (see p. 71). Drumstick allium flowers on

on leeks, frothy mounds of bright
yellow flowers on kale and pretty
cow-parsley type flowers on carrots –
flowering veg can be beautiful and will
be a magnet for bees and butterflies.

Borage
Borago officinalis

▶ Many herbs not only look
and taste great, they're useful
plants for pollinators too.

HERBS WITH FLOWER POWER: GROW A HERBAL NECTAR BAR

Bring in the bees by planting a pollinator-friendly
nectar bar in, or next to, your veg plot. There are hundreds of suitable
plants – some of them happen to taste great too, so why not plant a
multi-purpose herbal nectar bar? Choose a sunny spot and don't bother
adding compost to the soil as most herbs grow better and have stronger
flavours when planted in poor soil.

Fennel (*Foeniculum vulgare*)
A tall, feathery-fronded herb with
pretty yellow flowers in summer.
These are especially adored by
hoverflies. Every part of the plant
is edible – try using the pollen as
an edible garnish for soups.

**Rosemary (*Salvia rosmarinus,*
formerly *Rosmarinus officinalis*)**
An evergreen shrub with bluish-
purple flowers in spring and on
and off throughout the year.
Bees appreciate its long
flowering period.

**Oregano/Wild marjoram
(*Origanum vulgare*)** Pink flowered
varieties are especially loved by
bees and butterflies (they were
listed top of a study on bee-
friendly plants by the University of
Sussex). Delicious with tomatoes
and easier to grow than basil.

Borage (*Borago officinalis*) A great
source of nectar for insects and it's
perfect in a glass of Pimm's too!
Especially loved by honeybees
but will also benefit wild bees
and butterflies.

How can I increase my yields?

THE MOST PRODUCTIVE home veg plots can out-yield commercial farms considerably in terms of produce per unit of land. How do you make sure your veg plot is productive and maximise your yields in an eco-friendly way?

Keep your soil in good condition with lots of homemade garden compost. Always try to anticipate when patches of ground in your plot will become available so you can be ready to sow or plant something, to get the very best use of your space throughout the year.

Time and space

Aim to have as little bare soil in your veg patch as possible. Intercropping is a really useful technique that makes use of the gaps between certain crops to squeeze in quick-growing crops while there's space. For example, sow early lettuces in between your asparagus rows – they will have plenty of light until the canopy of the asparagus closes over in midsummer. By that time you will have harvested the lettuce anyway.

◀ Tomatoes, herbs and lettuce make good intercropping companions with asparagus.

Speedy radishes can give you a crop in the space between slower-growing cauliflowers, and so on.

Succession sowing helps avoid gluts and famines. Aim to sow small batches of crops such as salads every few weeks through the growing season. These can be grown in pots or modules so you can plant straight into the ground when one crop finishes – this is especially useful in late summer and means your young plants will have time to give a crop before winter.

Trying to predict gaps and being ready with seeds or plants to fill them is key for maximising productivity. If there's nothing you can or want to grow, sow a green manure or mulch the soil surface with garden compost or farmyard manure.

Technical help

Two man-made ways to increase yields are to get a greenhouse or polytunnel (see p. 130) and to use F1 hybrid seed. F1 vegetable seed is specifically bred for optimum, uniform results and high yields. However, it's more energy-intensive to produce and you can't save your own seed from F1 plants, so it's not necessarily the greenest option.

Sunflower
Helianthus spp.

Make use of all available space – there are crops that will grow in the shade such as redcurrants, and you can even grow pumpkins on a compost heap!

Grow with the flow

Grow what grows well for you. For example, if you have very acid soil, grow blueberries rather than cabbages, as they'll enjoy the conditions much more and give you much better harvests.

Ensure successful pollination

Lots of fruit and veg require pollination to produce a crop. Include pollinator-friendly plants such as herbs, sunflowers and pot marigolds (*Calendula officinalis*) – they'll bring joy to humans as well.

BOOSTING YOUR SOIL'S FERTILITY

Fertile soil is key to a productive vegetable garden, but it's not a case of the more fertiliser you apply, the more you'll be able to harvest. Be aware that throwing on lots of commercially produced 'general purpose' fertiliser can disrupt your soil's chemistry and disturb associations between plants and beneficial fungi (known as mycorrhizae).

The most environmentally-friendly way to increase your soil's fertility is to make lots of compost, and spread it as a mulch. Green manures, especially those in the legume family, are useful for adding fertility. Homemade

fertiliser, such as comfrey or nettle liquid feed is helpful too, particularly for tomatoes.

Remember that different fertilisers do different things – nitrogen-rich feeds such as pelleted chicken manure are good for leafy crops like brassicas, while potassium – potash – rich foods encourage flowering and fruiting so are perfect for crops such as chillies and sweet peppers.

Pelleted chicken manure

Is a wormery worth it?

THE IDEA OF HAVING A MULTI-STOREY worm wonderland outside your back door might not sound instantly appealing. But many people have them, so what's the draw? What benefits do they have for the environment – and for your garden?

Wormeries create some wonderful products with many uses in the garden. By having a wormery you can make your own environmentally-friendly fertiliser and soil improver that will really benefit your plants. They're particularly valuable if you want to make your own organic fertiliser and your garden is too small to produce enough waste to make a compost heap work properly.

'There's not a finer pet anywhere' says Amy Stewart, author of *The Earth Moved*, a 212-page biography of the earthworm. It seems a bold statement for a much-maligned creature. However, when you dig a bit deeper, you'll see that worms are pretty amazing creatures, and useful ones at that.

What is a wormery and what does it do?

Wormeries are devices for keeping a colony of worms in a confined area so they can be easily fed and the fertility they produce can be easily harvested. You feed the wormery with kitchen scraps such as vegetable peelings, eggshells and teabags. Bacteria then begin to break them down, and the worms feed on the bacteria and the scraps. It might sound offputting but it produces some of the best natural fertilisers in existence.

The basic format of a wormery is a series of stacking trays, filled in turn with kitchen waste. As the worms finish processing one tray, they move up to the next, leaving nutrient-rich castings and liquid to filter down. These castings contain useful amounts of nitrogen (which promotes leafy growth) and potassium (which promotes fruit and flowers). Liquid will collect at the bottom – many wormeries have a tap – and this is a potent tonic for your garden. Dilute it 1:10 with water and use it as a liquid fertiliser.

A range of material for a healthy wormery.

If I leave pests on vegetables, will I still get a crop?

IF YOU'RE SQUEAMISH about squishing or loath to liquidate the pests in your vegetable garden, can you still get usable harvests? Or is vegetable gardening all about do or die?

Older gardening books can sometimes portray the vegetable plot as something of a war zone. The options were to use poisonous chemicals or unpleasant means to physically dispatch the marauding insect life. Fortunately, times have changed and attitudes have softened.

Viewing your garden as just one small part of a bigger ecosystem can really change your perspective. The nefarious gardening ways of old really aren't the answer any more. So if your cabbages have a few caterpillars on them, you may as well leave them.

Most of the time, if you hold your nerve, wasps or blue tits will very happily take care of the caterpillars for you. Ladybirds will arrive to eat the aphids, and in turn help to nurture the next generation of predators to cope with the next onslaught of pests.

Spraying chemical pesticides on your plants is as likely to kill the predators as it is your pests. For severe infestations where no predators are in sight, you can either buy biocontrols (pest-destroying organisms, generally predatory or parasitic insects) or physically remove most pests by blasting them off with a hose.

Another less violent way to deal with vegetable pests is to use physical barriers, such as fine mesh or fleece. These are especially useful for preventing cabbage white caterpillars and carrot fly. Being plastic, they do have an environmental impact, so prolong their life by using them carefully, and washing and putting them away carefully at the end of each growing season.

Carrot fly
Chamaepsila rosae

Leaving a few pests on your vegetables will still allow you to get a crop, and should help support healthy populations of pest predators. If you garden in a way that attracts wildlife, these predators will never be too far away. It's just a case of holding your nerve until they arrive.

Can compost be re-used?

AT THE END OF THE GROWING SEASON, you've removed faded plants from their containers on your patio but there's still lots of compost left in the bottom of the pots. Should it go in the bin or compost heap? Or can it be re-used?

Re-using compost scores lots of eco points by helping spread the environmental impact of its manufacture, packaging and transport. There are a few things to watch out for though, to ensure you get the best results when re-using old compost.

▼ Compost can be re-used but you need to check it over for pests first, and be aware you may need to add fertiliser too.

In most cases, it's fine to re-use compost, although it's important to remember that after supporting plants for a season's growth it won't contain as many nutrients as freshly bought compost. So add some fertiliser or mix it with fresh compost, and check it over for pests as you go.

Re-using compost in containers

It's fine to re-use compost in containers, although for optimum growth, mix in some fresh compost, and add some fertiliser. General-purpose fertilisers are fine for most plants; but make sure you check old compost for any pests that may be lurking in it. Slow- or controlled-release fertilisers can be especially useful when you're re-using compost for long-lasting container plants such as topiary or shrubs.

Reusing compost in the garden

Putting spent compost from pots and containers in the compost heap is okay in small amounts. Try not to add too much at once, because, as it's already broken down, its presence will slow down the decomposition of the heap. So you might as well save yourself the effort and dig it straight into the soil.

Seed sowing

Avoid re-using compost when you sow your seeds. Any previously used compost may have accumulated harmful fungi, bacteria, weed seeds or pests, so it's always best to sow seeds in fresh compost and water them with tap water rather than from water butts until they've got at least four leaves.

TWO BADDIES TO WATCH OUT FOR IN OLD COMPOST

Vine weevils are the patio gardener's nemesis. They love laying their eggs in the compost of pot-grown plants. Once the grubs hatch they devour plant roots, causing wilting and sometimes even death. Vine weevil grubs are creamy white C-shaped maggots with shiny brown heads. Squish on sight, or use a biocontrol.

Slugs love potted plants too. Small slugs can often be found loitering around the bottom of the pot, close to the drainage holes. They will sometimes lay eggs in pots too. Look for pearly-white or yellowish clusters of small round eggs. Sometimes gardeners confuse these with slow-release fertiliser granules; however these are generally darker yellow-brown and you'll find them throughout the compost rather than in clusters.

Grub of vine weevil
Otiorhynchus sulcatus

Leopard slug
Limax maximus

Will a greenhouse earn its keep?

'GROWING UNDER COVER' or 'growing protected crops' sounds like a secret agent's way of gardening – but these descriptions are really just shorthand for cultivating plants in a greenhouse or polytunnel. Lots of gardeners do it, but do the benefits outweigh the costs of getting set up?

A greenhouse or polytunnel is a huge boost to anyone who loves gardening and enjoys growing their own food. You'll save a packet – literally – by helping reduce food miles and packaging. Consider buying a second-hand greenhouse and grow as many crops as you can in it for maximum benefit.

A greenhouse can seem like a big investment – not just in money but also in terms of garden space and the environmental resources needed to make it in the first place. However, a greenhouse will allow you to grow a wider variety of crops, over a longer period of the year. It will also give you bigger harvests per unit area of soil than growing in the open, so there are some definite advantages to growing under cover. Crops like tomatoes, cucumbers and basil go from being slightly risky outdoor crops in many parts of the country to pretty much guaranteed success.

The cheapest, greenest option is to buy a second-hand aluminium greenhouse. Be aware that you'll probably have to take it apart and reassemble it, which takes time and patience but is ultimately very rewarding. Greenhouses are especially useful on allotments as they have inbuilt gutters, making it easy to collect water in butts.

▼ Greenhouses make growing lots of different crops possible.

Warm and dry

One of the most joyful pleasures of gardening is to escape into a warm, dry greenhouse on a chilly day. Being surrounded by lush plants and flowers, and hearing the rain drum on the roof as you potter about has warmed many a gardener's heart over the years. The protected environment offered by growing under cover means you can grow lots more plants from seed, experiment with new things and generally take your gardening to the next level.

Grapes make a delicious greenhouse crop. The extra warmth means you'll have a greater chance of getting successful harvests.

No such thing as a bargain

Avoid cheap flimsy plastic greenhouses at all costs – the sort available as a kit online or at discount supermarkets. Not only are they an environmental disaster, they're actually really expensive in the long run. Their flimsy poles mean that they'll fall over in the first storm, and the plastic covers degrade quickly in sunlight. So they'll need replacing at least every couple of years, which quickly becomes expensive compared to longer-lasting alternatives.

GREENHOUSE OR POLYTUNNEL?

Resources: Greenhouses are more resource-heavy to make, particularly aluminium ones. However they last a lot longer than polytunnels. Both greenhouse glass and polytunnel covers are technically recyclable but aren't always accepted at kerbside collections.

Flexibility: Polytunnels are much easier to construct on sloping ground, and their extra height allows you to experiment with growing different crops. However, they're easier to damage, for example, by accidentally poking cane through the membrane.

Price: Initially greenhouses are much more expensive per unit area of growing space. However, as the coverings of polytunnels need to be replaced every 5–10 years, this difference diminishes over time.

Maintenance: Aluminium greenhouses are virtually maintenance free. A quick yearly wash is all that's needed. Polytunnels need cleaning too, and are more prone to damage from pets, storms, or canes and need repairing promptly.

Q How can I avoid gluts?

FUNNY ISN'T IT how familiarity can breed contempt? A courgette in June is a treat; but if you grow your own, sometimes by late August you'll be putting them on people's doorsteps, ringing the bell and running away. Are there ways to avoid this feast-or-famine situation or is it just an intrinsic part of vegetable growing?

Peas
Pisum sativum

Luckily there is a whole host of ways to avoid getting gluts in the vegetable garden. The most basic is to avoid sowing or planting too much of any one crop at any one time. For the quickest-growing crops like salad leaves and radishes, this will mean making a small sowing every few weeks in spring and summer.

For slightly slower-growing crops like carrots and beetroot you can make three sowings, one in early spring, one in late spring and then a final summer sowing. Do a similar thing with French beans and courgettes, make an early sowing under glass in late April or early May, then another one outdoors in June. That way you'll get a staggered crop over many months rather than just one overwhelming wave in August. Again, remember not to sow too many seeds at once.

Very hardy crops, such as shallots, onions, garlic, broad beans and peas, have both autumn and spring planting varieties. Grow some of both to spread your harvests. In fact, you can use different varieties of many crops to extend your harvesting season and avoid gluts. Everbearing strawberries and tall varieties of climbing peas such as 'Alderman' crop steadily all summer long; and there are early, mid- and late-season varieties of many fruits including apples, pears, plums and raspberries.

A The key to avoiding gluts is never to sow or plant too much of any one crop at any one time. You can stagger the sowing or planting times of many crops to make sure you have usable harvests over a long period. Try growing a few different varieties of the same crop to extend your harvesting period too.

WHAT TO DO IF YOU DO END UP WITH A GLUT

The best thing you can do with a glut is to spread the love. Share with friends, neighbours and food banks if they are able to accept donations of fresh produce. Crop swaps can be great fun on allotments; you never know what you might get in return and it can be a useful way to discover new crops that grow well in your area.

Freezing is a hugely useful way to deal with an overabundance of produce – finding some homegrown fruit and veg in the freezer can really brighten a dreary February day! Freeze in usable portions and always label and date everything so you can keep track of it.

Many crops freeze brilliantly: berries, beans, chard, apples and rhubarb are good examples. Blanch veg briefly in boiling water or steam to keep them fresh for longer. Most 'Mediterranean' type vegetables such as tomatoes, sweet peppers and courgettes don't freeze well individually but work brilliantly when cooked into stews, sauces or soups and then frozen.

 There are many ways to deal with a glut, from freezing to juicing to sharing with friends and neighbours.

Frozen cherries

Q **I want to keep honeybees, what should I know before I start?**

THE GENTLE BUZZ of busy bees happily pollinating your fruit, veg and flowers; the bright golden glow of honey dripping onto hot toast ... beekeeping can sound pretty seductive! But are there any hard truths to know about before you get going?

A Bees don't take up much space but need careful siting to make sure they don't cause problems for you or your neighbours. There are different types of hives and many styles of beekeeping. Do your research, join a beekeeping club and find out as much as you can before buying any equipment or trying to source bees.

Traditional beekeeping involves a 'moveable frame hive' – the bees build comb (where they lay eggs and store honey) on a series of frames contained within the hive. It's the beekeeper's job to inspect these over roughly weekly from April to August, checking the health of the colony and preventing swarming. By the time you've put on your bee suit, lit the smoker, inspected your frames and put everything back together, that's at least 30 minutes, every week.

Frames full of honey can be remarkably heavy – if you have a back injury this isn't for you. Honey harvesting is messy and laborious. It requires lots of equipment too – although you may be able to borrow or hire some if you join a local beekeeping club. You can join a club even if you don't have bees and it's a great way to learn. To keep bees on an allotment you must get agreement from the site representative and you should be a member of the British Beekeepers Association for insurance purposes.

Different approaches

There are as many different ways of beekeeping as there are beekeepers. The important thing is to do lots of research before you start. Many traditionalists will take as much honey as they can, and will be prepared to feed the bees with sugar-based products to get them through the winter. 'Natural' beekeepers have a lower impact approach, taking less honey but balancing this out with lower levels of interference with the bees, i.e. less work for the beekeeper.

Antisocial behaviour

Honeybees are generally docile creatures who will only sting if they feel under threat. However, you need to be aware of their flight path: as they zoom off from the hive entrance they will zoom into you if you get in their way, so make sure hives face away from busy areas, and place barriers such as fences or shrubs relatively close to the hive to make the bees fly up above head height. They will also defecate as they fly out of the hive, so don't site hives close to washing lines or parked cars.

IS KEEPING BEES GOOD FOR THE ENVIRONMENT?

While it might seem that keeping bees is a guaranteed win for nature, the truth isn't quite that simple. Honeybees are just one of around 270 native species of bee in the UK, and they're the only ones that live in such large colonies.

Having a hive containing many thousands of bees in your garden or allotment will undoubtedly improve pollination of your fruit and veg crops. However, such large numbers of bees inevitably compete with wild bees for nectar and pollen. Some wild bee species are endangered, whereas honeybees are comparatively very common.

In towns and cities, there may not be that many wild bees around anyway. If you live next to a nature reserve or wildlife site that is known for its wild bee populations, having a hive might impact those wild species and therefore is probably best avoided.

Is it greener to mix things up in the veg plot?

SHOULD A VEGETABLE PATCH just be for vegetables, weed-free and identical like soldiers on parade? Or does it make sense to jumble things up, grow flowers among the veg and generally loosen up a bit?

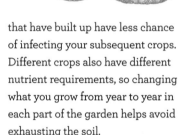

Squashes and pumpkins
Cucurbita

There is some scientific evidence to prove that mixing things up by growing certain plants together results in benefits to crop plants (see pp. 110–11). For example, certain flowers can attract pest predators. Growing herb fennel on your veg plot will not only give you several months of pretty flowers, they in turn will bring in lots of hoverflies, whose larvae eat lots of aphids. French marigolds (*Tagetes*) are another good example: they have long been grown next to tomatoes as they can help prevent root nematodes and other pests.

It pays to move your vegetables around the plot from year to year ('rotate' them). The basic theory is to divide most common crops into families; brassicas (cabbage, kale, cauliflower, etc.), alliums (onions, garlic, leeks), umbellifers (carrots, celery, parsnips), legumes (peas and beans) and nightshades (potatoes and tomatoes). Perennial crops like asparagus don't need to be rotated.

So, by not growing the same crop (or its close relatives) in the same place next year, any pests or diseases that have built up have less chance of infecting your subsequent crops. Different crops also have different nutrient requirements, so changing what you grow from year to year in each part of the garden helps avoid exhausting the soil.

A Mixing things up to avoid big monocultures (all the same crop) is a good idea, as is moving your annual crops round from year to year. Adding flowers, herbs and other useful plants will look pretty and help bring in beneficial wildlife. You are likely to see increased pollination, fewer pests and also fewer diseases.

Does vertical veg-growing work?

SHORT ON SPACE but keen to grow veg? Making use of vertical space in your garden can be a really handy way to maximise the efficiency of your space. But which crops are happy to head for the heavens rather than sprawling on the ground?

Vertical veg growing is a useful way to maximise your harvests from even the tiniest gardens. There are lots of climbing crops that will be only too happy to festoon arches, wander up wigwams and grow on walls. Try colourful and tasty climbing French beans, climbing courgettes or even exotic cucamelons.

▶ Thanks to modern breeding and a range of different rootstocks and pruning techniques, you can fit a fruit tree into even the tiniest garden.

Climbing French beans come in a range of colours and pod shapes – purple, yellow and green; flat or pencil-podded. If the pods become tough, just leave them to dry on the plant – they're delicious soaked and cooked (they're the same species as baked beans).

The classic example of vertical veg growing is a teepee of runner beans. Most gardeners leave it at that, but there are lots of other veg that are quite happy to climb canes, trellises, arches or whatever other support you can give them.

There are climbing varieties of courgettes and climbing peas. Mini pumpkins and squashes look great scrambling up archways (although be prepared to support the fruit if they need it). Cucumbers and cucamelons grow brilliantly up wires along the back end of a greenhouse.

Large-scale vertical farming

Vertical farming is a recent development. Crops such as salads, microgreens and herbs are grown indoors in warehouses, shipping containers and even abandoned train tunnels! The plants grow in controlled hydroponic or aeroponic conditions with LED lighting. Its promoters claim massive yields – up to ten times that of conventional farming per unit area. The space-saving nature and lack of need for good soil make vertical farming ideally suited to supplying food in urban areas.

Chapter 4

Wildlife Back-up

Do bees need weeds?

BEASTLY BRAMBLES, thuggish thistles, incorrigible ivy... some of the wild plants we call weeds have pretty mean reputations when seen through human eyes. But how do bees see them? Is a weed just a weed to man or also to beast?

Bumblebee
Bombus hypnorum

Humans are just whippersnappers in evolutionary terms. Honeybees have been on the wing in search of flowers for around 35 million years, while we (in our current form) have been plodding about for just a couple of hundred thousand. That's less than 1 per cent of the time bees have existed. What's more, we've only been calling plants 'weeds' since the dawn of agriculture in the last few millennia of that time. Do bees care that we think a plant is a weed? No!

Weeds are often the first plants to rush in after man has bulldozed, dug or paved over our precious earth. The fact that they can turn such wounds into sweet nectar for bees means they deserve a little respect. Many weeds are valuable bee plants, and will help to turn even barren wastelands into an insect paradise.

Are the plants we corral into this definition, unloved and unwanted by humans, wanted and loved by bees? There is no unifying biological characteristic to weeds, other than that they're 'plants in the wrong place'. A flower is a flower, whether it's a buddleia growing in the cracks of an abandoned building or a beautiful cornflower in an organic meadow. The fact that it's there at all is what matters to bees.

◀ Many common garden weeds are a rich source of nectar and pollen for bees and other insects.

Seasonal treasures

Some non-native weeds can be particularly valuable for bees as they do something that many indigenous plants don't: they provide abundant nectar in late summer and early autumn. There can be a bit of a gap in what beekeepers call the 'nectar flow' at this time and buddleia can help fill it.

What about lawns?

Perfect bowling green lawns might look pleasing to the human eye but to bees they might as well be green-coloured concrete. If you care at all about bees, don't treat your

Meadow buttercup
Ranunculus acris

lawn with herbicides (avoid any product with the word 'weed' in the name), and consider leaving parts of it uncut for a few months in spring and early summer. Your turf will literally blossom with nectar-rich daisies, clover and dandelions – and the bees will love you for it.

UNLIKELY HERO WEEDS FOR BEES

Some of these weeds are pretty unpopular – and prolific growers. This information is supplied solely to demonstrate that even the most irritating plants can have some redeeming qualities:

Dandelion (*Taraxacum officinale*)
This tenacious weed is often the scourge of a clear lawn, but its flowers are a rich source of pollen and nectar. Each yellow head has hundreds of smaller flowers containing vital nutrients for bees.

White clover (*Trifolium repens*)
This nitrogen-fixing legume attracts parasitoid wasps – a great boon if you have a problem with aphids, scales, and whiteflies.

Sycamore (*Acer pseudoplatanus*)
Many trees are really valuable for bees and sycamore is no exception. It provides copious nectar in May; some beekeepers add extra frames to their hives when sycamore is flowering to cope with the extra honey.

Q What use are slugs?

THEY HAVE TENTACLES, slime, tens of thousands of teeth and an unerring instinct to find the most delicate and precious of a gardener's newly-planted seedlings. Slugs sound like the perfect enemy. But are they really as bad as we think they are? And are they all as bad as each other?

2

1

A

Believe it or not, most slugs are actually good for the garden. Most don't eat live plants at all – they're nature's cleaners, helping tidy up all kinds of garden waste. There are only a few species that damage live plants, and there are some that eat other slugs. All of them are an important part of the food chain for garden wildlife.

Slugs are a hardworking bunch. You could call them nature's cleaners. There are around 40 species in Britain and most of them spend most of their time harmlessly chomping away on dead or dying material, helping recycle nutrients in the garden and making them much more accessible to plants. Having slugs in the compost heap is actually a good thing!

Only a few species of slug are pests. But even these have their benefits. Contrary to common belief, they do eat weeds too – it's just that gardeners tend not to notice weed seedlings disappearing. They are also a valuable food source for wildlife such as hedgehogs, birds and toads.

▼ Despite their occasionally annoying appetites for favourite plants, slugs have some surprising redeeming qualities.

GOOD SLUG: BAD SLUG

1. Leopard slug (*Limax maximus*) (also known as the great grey slug) Undoubtedly the gardener's slug superstar. With its cool spotty pattern and tendency to eat any slugs (and even snails) it encounters, it's definitely one to let live.

2. Spanish slug (*Arion vulgaris*) These can grow into 15cm (6 in) whoppers and have an appetite to match. Their colour varies from light brownish-orange to dark chocolate brown but they can easily be confused with other species. They eat almost anything and everything.

3. Green cellar slug (*Limacus maculatus*) Mostly eats mould and algae, helping to recycle plant nutrients, so it is actually a gardener's ally. Unless, that is, it gets a scent of pet food, in which case it may overstep the mark.

4. Grey field slug (*Deroceras reticulatum*) A very common and variable species that makes quite a nuisance of itself. Its colour can vary from white to almost black; distinguished by its dark speckles and milky mucus.

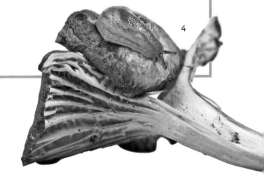

Not quite vegan

You might think that slugs have an entirely plant-based diet – however, they have much wider tastes than just your lettuce seedlings; some are detritivores (scavengers that eat everything from fallen leaves to dead animals and excrement), herbivores (eat your plants) and, interestingly, omnivores and carnivores who'll happily eat other slugs.

To pellet or not to pellet

The unfortunate thing about slug pellets is they kill all slugs. Even the useful ones, which want nothing more than to recycle your garden rubbish. They can also poison other wildlife like hedgehogs and birds. Use pellets with caution, if at all.

Which bees might I be able to see in my garden?

WHEN YOU SAY THE WORD 'BEE', most people think of a stripy thing that makes honey. Or perhaps a big buzzy bumblebee, bumbling about on a spring day. However, there are around 2,000 species of bee in Europe. Many are frequent visitors to gardens – how can you tell which is which?

Mason bees, mining bees, carder bees – the world of garden bees is much broader than just the well-known honey and bumblebees. If you plant plenty of flowers and avoid using garden chemicals, you may well see a surprising number of different bee species visit your garden.

It may not surprise you that there are about 90 species of mammal found in Britain, but few people would know that there are almost three times that number of native bee species. Although there's only one honeybee in the UK, there are 25 kinds of bumblebee and more than 250 different solitary bees. The term 'solitary' simply means that they live as individuals, as opposed to 'social' bees which live as a colony and have a queen who lays all the eggs.

The word solitary is a bit of a misnomer though, as solitary bees can sometimes live and breed in quite close proximity to each other. They have a fascinating range of habits. Leafcutter bees make intricate nests from pieces of leaves and flowers, while mining bees excavate deep chambers in the soil and mason bees live in cracks in walls. The more you look, the more you'll be drawn into the fascinating world of these important and incredibly diverse creatures.

Solitary bee tucked up inside a hollow reed stem. Making a simple 'bug hotel' (see p. 172) will help these pollinators.

SIX COMMON GARDEN BEES

Take time out on a sunny summer day and get to know the bees that visit your garden!

1. Garden bumblebee (*Bombus hortorum*) Common in gardens, loves tubular flowers such as foxgloves as it has a very long tongue (which can be as long as its entire body!). Three yellow bands and a furry white bottom.

2. Tree bumblebee (*Bombus hypnorum*) Another fluffy-looking bee with an orange-brown thorax (middle), a black abdomen and a white tail. Often nests in disused bird boxes or in roofs and is a useful pollinator of fruit bushes.

3. Honeybee (*Apis mellifera*) Small and slender compared to a bumblebee. Honeybees have a furry thorax but the abdomen is much smoother than most other native bees, with brownish-yellow and black stripes.

4. Common carder bee (*Bombus pascuorum*) Small and fluffy, quite variable in colour. It tends to have a ginger thorax and beige-brown abdomen, sometimes with pronounced black stripes.

5. Red mason bee (*Osmia bicornis*) About the size of a honeybee but fat, furry and ginger, with a black boxy head. Nests in a range of sites, including bee hotels and bare soil faces, and an excellent pollinator.

6. Red-tailed bumblebee (*Bombus lapidarius*) A very bright, scarlet red tail contrasts strongly with the rest of the abdomen which is jet-black. Social, nests in old mouse burrows or underneath rocks.

Which plant varieties are best for wildlife?

A ROSE IS A ROSE IS A ROSE, RIGHT? **Well, depending on the name of that rose it might be a bee banquet – or as barren as a piece of cardboard. When it comes to providing pollen, nectar and other food sources for wildlife – all flowers are not created equal. So how do you spot the difference?**

When you're choosing which varieties of a particular plant to grow, avoid those with double flowers. That way you'll ensure that there's pollen, nectar and potentially fruits and seeds for wildlife too. Some varieties naturally produce more food for wildlife than others – check out the RHS Plants for Pollinators lists, and do some careful observation next time you're at the garden centre.

what we call a 'double' flower – where most of its reproductive parts are replaced by petals, we save and treasure it, despite the fact biologically it's a bit useless.

Most double flowers are pretty much infertile. They're no good for bees and other pollinating insects – those extra petals make the flower showier and longer lasting, but they come at the expense of pollen- and nectar-bearing organs that supply insects with food.

Rugosa rose
Rosa rogosa

There's a simple rule of thumb you can apply when trying to work out which varieties of a certain plant will be best for wildlife. Avoid the ones with double flowers. In nature, flowers are there to be pollinated and set seed as quickly as possible. As gardeners, we like to slow the show down a little, even stop it entirely sometimes. So when we find a plant that accidentally produces

ARE ALL FLOWERS EQUAL? WHAT THE SCIENCE SAYS

A 2013 study by scientists at the University of Sussex suggested that common garden flowers vary a hundredfold in their attractiveness to pollinating insects. What mattered was the individual characteristics of the variety, more than whether it was 'highly bred' or not.

Hybrid varieties such as the lavender 'Grosso' were actually more attractive to wildlife than species, such as French lavender, *Lavandula stoechas*. Flower shape matters a great deal in some cases, such as dahlias. Open-flowered cultivars such as 'Bishop of Llandaff' were consistently more attractive to pollinators than those with pompom (an extreme form of double flower) blooms such as 'Franz Kafka'.

Rose
Rosa cv.

Double flowers, such as this rose cultivar, often contain very little pollen or nectar.

The other problem with double flowers is that, being largely infertile, they don't provide berries or seeds for wildlife either. The vigorous rambling rose (*Rosa filipes*) 'Kiftsgate' is great for wildlife as its simple, single flowers are very much open for business to any passing pollinator. After successful fertilisation the flowers are followed by generous sprays of scarlet berries (hips), to the delight of blackbirds and a host of other garden wildlife in the cold winter months. Its spiny, rampant growth also makes ideal bird nesting territory. At the other end of the scale, an almost infertile, restrained, double-flowered hybrid tea rose like *Rosa* 'Blue Moon' does next to nothing for wildlife.

Single flowers with their open centres are designed to be attractive to pollinating wildlife.

Which bees need what when?

THERE ARE MORE THAN 200 SPECIES of bee in the UK and at least a dozen are commonly found in gardens. While some are 'social', and others are 'solitary' – what do these different lifestyles mean for bees' needs?

Bees have a far more pronounced yearly cycle than we do, so their needs vary greatly according to the season. A honeybee colony can grow to about 60,000 individuals in midsummer, before dwindling to as few as 10,000 in late winter. Many solitary bees (such as mason bees and mining bees) become almost invisible to us over winter – the previous season's adults all die off and the next generation overwinters in cocoons away from view. The main thing that they – along with bumblebees – need, is safe nesting spots such as bee hotels, long grass and corners of the garden that aren't too tidy during their nesting season.

Bees need food and homes. The more pollen- and nectar-rich plants you can provide in your garden the better, especially if you aim for year-round flowers. Check out the RHS Plants for Pollinators lists online (rhs.org.uk/plantsforpollintors) for planting ideas by season. Bee hotels and bare ground or earth help provide homes for wild bees.

▼ ▶ Honeybees have a strict social hierarchy, and the number of workers (females) and drones (males) changes dramatically throughout the course of a year.

Worker (female)

Drone (male)

Queen

A year of bees' needs

Spring – Bees need lots of flowers, especially pollen-rich ones, to help them feed their young. Bare earth is handy for nesting sites and as material for some solitary bees.

Summer – Plant plenty of different flowers to attract a range of different bee species. Some bees have longer tongues than others so they can pollinate different shapes of flower.

Autumn – For honeybees, nectar becomes especially important now as brood rearing decreases and the colony lays down honey stores for the winter.

Winter – Honeybees and some bumblebees will fly in mild spells, appreciating any winter-flowering plants in your garden.

Bieberstein's crocus
Crocus speciosus

TOP PLANTS TO HELP BEES THROUGH TOUGH TIMES

Bee-bee tree (*Tetradium daniellii*) A lovely medium-sized tree that is covered in white, fragrant flowers in late summer, which can be really useful to help honeybees make ample stores of honey to see them through winter.

Ivy (*Hedera helix*) Many people are surprised to learn that ivy is actually a brilliant bee plant. It flowers in autumn, giving abundant nectar which bees appreciate to help them survive the winter. Ivy flowers only appear on established plants which have become shurbby ('arborescent').

Goat willow (*Salix caprea*) One of our earliest willows to bloom, the goat willow's fluffy catkins provide an excellent early source of pollen. Protein-rich and abundant, bees feed it to their young, so having some of these willows around is a big boost.

Crocus All species and hybrids are loved by bees. *Crocus tommasinianus* naturalises well in lawns while the big Dutch hybrids provide lots of pollen and nectar, and a warm place for early bumblebees to rest.

Q What makes a meadow?

SOFT GRASS studded with jewel-like wildflowers and alive
with the chirping of crickets, the buzz of bees and butterflies
fluttering by... it's a seductive image and one that many wildlife
gardeners have tried to copy over the years. But what are the
secret ingredients? And is it an easy scene to re-create?

A true meadow is a rare sight these
days. The wildflower-rich grassy
turf so many of us dream of depends
on two things. The first is having
relatively poor soil, so that the flowers
aren't overrun by vigorous grasses.
Traditional meadows were cut, and
the cuttings removed as hay, which
over the years reduced the fertility
of the land. Secondly, the timing of
the cut is important: generally hay

A simple definition of meadow
is that it's a combination of
flowering plants and grasses.
There are two ways to
approach making a meadow
in your garden. If your soil
is fertile, make an annual
meadow by digging and
sowing seed every year. If
your soil is poor, change your
lawnmowing habits and your
lawn can become a meadow
all by itself.

▼ Many plants that
we now think of as
treasured wildflowers
were once common
weeds of arable fields
or grazing land.

meadows were cut between mid-July and September, and were often then grazed until early spring. This allowed wildflowers to bloom and seed undisturbed in spring and early summer.

There is another type of 'meadow' – a re-creation of an old-fashioned arable field that gets ploughed every year (hay meadows are never, ever, ploughed). Poppies, cornflowers, corn marigolds and so on make a colourful, annual display. Although it's not strictly a meadow, it's much easier to create and will succeed on richer soils (most garden soil is too fertile for a true wildflower meadow to work well). Annual ornamental grasses such as greater quaking grass (*Briza maxima*) and bunny's tails (*Lagurus ovatus*) look wonderful mixed in with the flowers – or you can play meadow roulette by sowing bird seed and seeing what comes up!

WHICH KIND OF MEADOW IS RIGHT FOR ME?

Both types of meadow need full sun to do well. They also need to be left, not be walked on by people or pets. If your garden is small, make a mini-meadow to one side. In larger plots you can mow a path through the middle or convert part of your lawn.

If your grass is always thick and lush, and your only weeds are dandelions, you'll be best off sticking to an annual meadow as the chances are your soil will be too fertile. Dig over the ground and sow cornfield or pictorial meadow seed mixes each year in spring.

On lawns that seem to be more daisies, speedwell and clover than grass, you're on to a winner. It's already trying to become a wildflower meadow! Cut the edges and any pathways through regularly, but otherwise leave the mower in the shed between March and August.

Should I ration food for wildlife?

YOU WANT TO BE KIND to your garden visitors to give them the best chance possible – but can you end up harming wildlife by putting out too much food? What about bringing in undesirables?

Feed wildlife such as birds carefully and consistently. Feeding lots and then suddenly stopping could do more harm than not feeding at all. Putting out too much food risks it going off, or attracting vermin, such as rats. The most sustainable way to provide sustenance is to plant lots of different seed- and berry-bearing plants to give natural food sources.

▶ Planting berrying or seed-bearing plants is the most eco-friendly way to feed wildlife.

Having a bird feeder or bird table brings a lot of joy to gardeners. Cheeky blue tits love gorging on peanuts and robins are crazy for mealworms that they can easily be tamed to eat from your hand. Lucky gardeners with local hedgehog populations will leave cat food out for their hogs.

Generally, wildlife won't over-eat. It's more likely that humans will over-feed and some will be left over. This is a problem because it can either spoil and become harmful to wildlife, or it will attract vermin. If you're feeding in the open, for example on bird tables, try to only to put out enough food so that the birds will have picked it clean by the end of the day. Human food such as table scraps is also more likely to attract rats so is best avoided. The best thing to do is grow plants that provide natural food sources such as berries and seeds.

SEEDS AND BERRIES

Berrying shrubs are a great source of food for birds: try cotoneasters, hawthorns and berberis. Seeds are valuable too, try to include some sunflowers, teasels or ornamental thistles, such as *Cirsium rivulare*.

Is a tiny pond worth it?

IT'S OFTEN SAID that the single best thing you can do to attract wildlife to your garden is to add water. But what if you've only got space for a tiny pond, barely bigger than a washing-up bowl? Is that enough to make a difference to the birds, bees and other creatures that call our gardens home?

Any water you add to your garden will have some value for wildlife: it could be a source of water to drink, somewhere to bathe or an entire habitat in itself.

Belfast sinks, half barrels or even old washing-up bowls can make great mini-ponds. Thoroughly clean them, add a layer of washed gravel at the bottom and fill with rainwater. Plant up with native aquatic plants, such as hornwort to oxygenate the water, and marginal plants like water forget-me-nots and marsh marigolds. Add an escape route in the form of a piece of untreated wood half-submerged in the water, resting on the rim, which will help any creatures that accidentally fall in to get out again.

Even the smallest amount of water in your garden will make a difference for wildlife, whether it's a takeaway tub converted into a bee drinker or a Belfast sink patio pond. Mini ponds can be hugely rewarding as they offer the chance to watch up close as a whole different ecosystem develops over time.

MAKING A BEE DRINKER

The tiniest water feature of all could be a bee drinker. Simply take a shallow container, such as a plant saucer or clean takeaway tub, and fill it with a layer of pebbles. Add water so that the pebbles are half submerged. Place in a sunny spot and grateful bees will soon fly in for a drink.

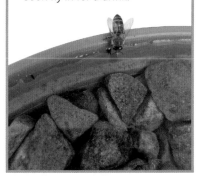

With careful planting, can I feed the birds all year round?

FEEDING THE BIRDS with home-grown food scores lots of eco points. What's more, many bird-friendly shrubs are appreciated by humans too for their colourful displays of berries. But can garden planting help feed the birds all year round?

The main sources of natural plant-based bird food in the garden are berries and seeds. Some berrying shrubs and especially trees produce enormous quantities of fruit, which can be really useful for birds. It's best to plant a range of different plants to provide food over as long a period as possible. Hawthorns (*Crataegus* spp. and hybrids) and crab apples (*Malus* spp. and hybrids) are particularly valuable; the twiggy, spiny growth of hawthorns is especially valuable for nesting sites. Amelanchiers (also known as juneberries or serviceberries) give early crops of berries and have lovely spring blossom too.

By choosing your plants carefully, and being prepared to store some seedheads for use later on, you can feed the birds year-round just from the plants in your garden. However, for most people it's probably worth buying at least some food, especially in late winter and spring.

Birds also love seeds. Thistles are a particularly useful group for providing seeds, and before you throw your hands up in horror, there are some very nice ones for garden use that aren't too invasive or spiny. Sunflowers are easy to grow and birds feed on the seeds. Dry the whole ripe heads in late summer and autumn to save the seeds (store them in a mouse-proof place) for feeding the birds in late winter and early spring when other food sources have run out.

Crab apple
Malus sylvestris

Omnivores

Don't forget that birds don't just eat seeds or berries. Many have quite broad-ranging diets. For example, blue tits will happily eat peanuts from feeders in winter, but in summer they'll equally enjoy aphids and caterpillars. Avoiding using insecticides will help ensure there are adequate natural food sources, as will growing insect-friendly plants like nasturtiums.

Thistle
Carduus spp.

▶ Thistles might not be very people-friendly but they're great for birds and other wildlife.

Hawthorn
Crataegus spp.

GROW YOUR OWN BIRD FOOD

Teasel (*Dipsacus fullonum*) A striking-looking native wildflower that grows up to 2m (7 ft) tall. It bears large spiky flowerheads that bloom in concentric rings, before becoming filled with small seeds which are much enjoyed by goldfinches.

Hawthorns (*Crataegus*) These are wonderfully wildlife-friendly small trees. The native may blossom (*C. monogyna*) along with the American cockspur thorn (*C. persimilis*) and others species have bee-friendly blossom followed by lots of small red fruits in autumn.

Crab apples (*Malus sylvestris*) Many varieties including 'John Downie' are also good small garden trees. Birds love eating crab apples straight from the tree or pecking at fallen fruit later in the winter.

Sunflowers (*Helianthus annuus*) Easy to grow and the nutritious, oil-rich seeds of these giant annual plants are much loved by birds. Can be cut and stored for later use. Grow a row or two in your veg patch.

Will simple neglect create a wildlife garden?

IF WILD IS BEST FOR WILDLIFE, surely all you have to do to make your garden more wildlife friendly is abandon it completely?

First, it depends what your garden is like before it gets neglected. If it was just lawn, all that will be created will be an overgrown lawn – good for some insect species, but a desert for others. Second, what are the gardens around yours like? Are they host to a variety of wildlife that will expand into your garden, or are the insects, mammals and amphibians going to have to overcome more obstacles to get to your space? The more diverse habitats around your garden, the more variety of wildlife you will see in yours. Also, bear in mind the neighbours – they may not appreciate you leaving your garden completely wild, and the potential effect on house prices.

Neglect will create the opportunity for more wildlife to call a garden home – up to a point. For the greatest variety of species, however, it is better to manage the garden to an extent, to offer the most variety and number of potential habitats.

▼ Floral variety is key for garden fauna for as well as the gardener. Allow for diverse habitats and be less fastidious to create a wildlife-friendly garden.

CREATING A WILDLIFE-FRIENDLY GARDEN

Actively creating a wildlife-friendly garden means designing features to create benefits for a range of species as well as making it a more attractive place for you to spend time. However, there are a few simple steps – small individual actions of neglect – that can also incorporate a variety of wildlife habitats and encourage the birds and minibeasts to make your garden home:

• Leave the lawn to grow longer. It can still be cut, but allowing a lusher sward rather than cutting it as short as a bowling green will allow more insects to live there – and encourage the birds that feed on them. If possible, leave one section completely uncut.

• Alternatively, sow wildflowers and herbs into the lawn for a mini-wildflower meadow; flowers will attract a greater diversity of insects than just grass.

• Don't tidy the borders until late winter, as the fallen leaves and hollow stems will provide hiding places for bugs and amphibians in the coldest months. Piles of dry leaves left in corners are also useful hibernating spots for mammals and amphibians.

• Let plants self-seed into paving cracks – they will provide hiding places for insects.

• Don't mend the fence – a small gap in the fence or wall either side of the garden allows hedgehogs to pass through.

• Allow nettles to grow in a corner of the garden, to provide egg-laying sites for butterflies and food for their larvae.

• Don't clear away all the garden debris – a log pile, a dead hedge, or a compost heap (or all three) – make great wildlife habitats.

Which species love shade?

YOUR GARDEN DOESN'T GET MUCH SUN, but you want to add some wildlife-friendly planting. What kind of insects and animals could help with a more shaded habitat?

Plenty of wildlife species will thrive in a shaded garden – anything that lives in a woodland for example – and often species that don't do so well in a sunny wildlife garden. Shaded gardens can provide food, shelter and cover for many insects and larger animals too, such as hedgehogs.

▼ Shady gardens usually contain plenty of trees – and leaf litter is an ideal foraging ground for hedgehogs.

What kind of shade?

First, establish why the garden is shady. Is it permanent shade, caused by neighbouring trees or buildings? Is the shade being caused by trees or a hedge on your own plot? Are the trees evergreen, casting shade all year round, or are they deciduous, letting in more light in spring? Is the shade complete, or dappled? Does it cover the whole garden all the time, or move around the garden through the day? Knowing the answers to these questions by simply observing the garden through the day and over the year will best inform any new planting or habitat creation in the garden to make it more attractive to wildlife.

A SHADED WILDLIFE GARDEN

Any garden will already be home to plenty of wildlife, even if it's not immediately obvious. To make it as attractive as possible to a diverse range of creatures, create a variety of food and shelter options. Visiting other shaded gardens and local woodlands can be a good source of ideas, but aiming for a woodland edge feel, with lighter and darker areas, means the garden has plenty of variety for both you and the wildlife.

Large trees Home to insects and birds as well as small mammals such as bats.

Small trees Blossom and berries provide nectar for insects and food for birds; supplement this by hanging bird feeders in the trees.

Mid-storey planting Flowers and berries on shrubs add another layer of food and also cover for larger wildlife like hedgehogs to move around undisturbed.

Understorey planting Spring flowers such as pulmonaria, primroses, bluebells and wood anemones provide nectar early in the season for bees and other insects.

Leaf litter This is home and food to worms, millipedes, slugs and snails; it also offers shelter to frogs, toads and slow worms.

Log pile Woodlice also love dead wood.

Stumpery Rotting wood is a haven for centipedes, beetles and the smaller bugs they feast on.

Pond A pond does best in some sunlight, but if it's possible, it will add another habitat to the garden, home to water insects such as damselflies and amphibians like frogs, toads and newts as well as provide a water source for birds and mammals.

Climbers Walls that are casting shade don't have to be bare: a shade-tolerant climber such as common ivy will provide shelter for birds and insects; nectar-rich flowers for bees and other insects; and berries for the birds.

▶ Old tree stumps are brilliant habitats for a variety of insects and invertebrates. Grow shade-loving ferns around them to create a stumpery garden.

Can I have a tidy wildlife garden?

YOU'D LIKE TO ATTRACT MORE WILDLIFE to your garden, but don't want to turn the lawn into a meadow or have overgrown borders and nettle patches. How can you keep a tidy garden and help wildlife at the same time?

Changes to the garden

Adding a pond is one of the best things to do for wildlife, and one that is completely compatible with a tidy garden. Just remember to add a ramp so creatures can get out safely if it has straight sides.

Instead of a nettle patch (which is excellent for butterflies), plant annuals, shrubs and perennials that provide a long season of nectar-rich flowers. When buying a new plant for the garden, choosing something that will add flowers at a time when the rest of the garden is less floriferous will benefit you and the wildlife.

Add some homes, such as a hedgehog house, bird boxes and bug hotels, and a bird feeder or two.

Use an open compost heap if you have space, as this allows more creatures to access it than the enclosed plastic types: well-managed heaps

Making a garden wildlife-friendly doesn't mean that the garden needs to look untidy or completely wild, but there are some places and tasks that can be changed in a minor way to better benefit the wildlife in the garden.

can be home to slow worms and grass snakes as well as all manner of insect and arthropod life.

Nature abhors a vacuum – planting up too great a patch of bare soil beneath shrubs with mat-forming perennials such as alpine strawberries, pulmonaria, sweet violets, alchemilla or periwinkle gives shelter and food to insects and other wildlife as well as reducing the need to weed.

▼ Careful planting choices will help wildlife such as this grass snake in the garden.

▶ Providing feeding stations for insects and birds doesn't have to mean an untidy garden.

Changes to gardening methods

To help attract wildlife to the garden, it can be useful to distinguish between tidy and fastidious. A tidy wildlife garden can have cut edges, a mown lawn and well-pruned shrubs, but it's important not to be too tidy (don't mow the grass every week) so that a range of wildlife can find an undisturbed home in your garden.

Cutting back herbaceous perennials in late winter/early spring rather than autumn is a simple way to help insects and birds: many beneficial minibeasts such as ladybirds will find a winter home in the dry, hollow stems, and the birds will appreciate the food from the seedheads. Plus, the heads, and particularly grasses, can look attractive, on a frosty morning.

Don't clear away all the autumn leaves and branches from pruning – leaving a pile of leaves and a small log pile in a quiet corner will provide more winter habitats. (Do remove everything that is diseased though.)

Leave some fallen fruit in the orchard and/or soft fruit garden – birds and wasps will feast on it.

Allowing some of the weeds – such as dandelions – to flower will mean bees benefit from the nectar, and they can still be removed before they set seed.

WARNING BELL

Birds and cats don't mix well in the garden – if your cat is likely to stalk and try to catch the birds you want to attract, simply putting a bell on its collar will help keep the birds safe, as well as keeping pets indoors from dusk until dawn.

Can I treat bugs with bugs?

Is it possible to order bugs online that are then watered into the soil to help get rid of pests? How does this work? Are there other kinds of bugs that eat bugs?

Your garden will already be host to a number of predatory insects, but it is possible to boost their numbers by buying in more. Their effectiveness in dealing with a pest problem depends on the type of bug and where it is released.

Using an insect's or other organism's natural predators to control a garden pest is called biological control. (Sprays are one form of control, physical control is picking off the insects yourself or using a barrier.)

Nematodes

Nematodes are microscopic soil-living organisms. Some feed on decaying matter, keeping the soil healthy, others feed on plant roots and are pests themselves. A third group are predatory and carnivorous, eating other nematodes and infecting soil-dwelling creatures such as insect larvae with fatal bacteria, and these are the type that can be used as a biological control. Nematodes need damp soil to work effectively. They can be bought in a pack that is mixed with water and applied to the soil with a watering can. There are nematodes that can help to control vine weevils (grubs/larvae) and slugs.

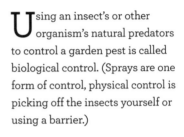
Nematodes can be mixed with water to add to the soil, where they will predate on soil pests.

Parasites

Other bugs can be controlled using parasitoid insects, which work by infecting the pest with a parasite that then kills it. They work best in greenhouses and are introduced usually in spring, and before a pest infestation gets out of hand, as the parasitoid population needs time to multiply before it can be truly effective. *Encarsia formosa* is an example of a parasitoid control, which is used against glasshouse whitefly. The control bugs can be ordered online and then released into the greenhouse.

Predators

It is thought that a single ladybird can eat up to 50,000 aphids during its lifetime. Both the larvae and the adults are voracious predators and are an excellent help in the garden, but other bugs such as hoverflies, lacewing flies and wasps (both the common wasp and solitary wasps) also predate on aphids. Attract them to the garden by planting umbelliferous and/or brightly coloured flowers, such as yarrow, fennel and pot marigolds.

In a greenhouse setting, it is also possible to buy and release predatory bugs (including species of ladybirds) that will eat pests, such as the predatory mite *Phytoseiulus persimilis* that will attack greenhouse red spider mites.

▶ As omnivores, the blackbird's diet includes insects, worms and snails, as well as fruits and seeds.

Blackbird
Turdus merula

NATURAL CONTROL

Blue tits and other birds also love to eat aphids – attracting them to the garden with a bird feeder in the winter will mean they stick around in the summer to eat the aphids. Using natural predators to keep control of pests is just one aspect of cultivating a healthy garden, and looking after the plants will mean they are less likely to get infested in the first place. It is also necessary to tolerate a low level of pest infestation in order to keep the beneficial insects in the garden as well – if there is no food for them at all, they will find it elsewhere.

Is shaded water good for anything?

YOU'D REALLY LIKE TO PUT A POND in your garden as you know they are great for wildlife, but the only possible site is mostly shaded. Will a pond be any good there? What wildlife might like a shaded pond?

Ponds in complete shade throughout the day become stagnant, because the oxygenating plants in the water are unable to work properly without enough sunlight. A pond that is in complete shade for only part of the day but in the sun the rest of the time, has only half of its surface permanently shaded or is in only dappled shade, will be able to function as a normal wildlife pond. Just use more shade-tolerant water plants (unfortunately water lilies prefer full sun) and be sure to scoop out as many fallen leaves from the surface as possible in autumn.

Ideally a wildlife pond will have at least half of its surface in the sun, but this means half can be in the shade, so it is possible. Wholly shaded ponds tend not to do so well at attracting wildlife, but a hoverfly lagoon (see box) can be shaded and still provide some breeding grounds for these beneficial insects.

▶ Bog gardens are ideal for a range of plants that thrive at the water's edge, such as irises and marsh marigolds.

Marsh marigold
Caltha palustris

Bog gardens

Instead of a pond, why not plant a bog garden? They will do well in a more shaded part of the garden, provided the right plants are used, and can still be a source of food and shelter for a range of wildlife including amphibians.

A bog garden can be created by digging out an area of soil and, essentially, making a leaky pond, either by using puddling clay but not puddling it completely (p. 180) or by re-using an old, leaking pond area or liner. It's important that the soil is rich and moist but that stagnant water is not allowed to collect, otherwise the plants will drown. Good plants for a bog garden include gunneras, hostas, ferns, primulas, irises, dogwood and willow.

Common toad
Bufo bufo

A HOVERFLY LAGOON

Hoverflies lay their eggs in stagnant water, so providing a place for them to do that will help increase their numbers in your garden.

Unfortunately, a lagoon is not the most attractive of ponds, but they can be as small as a pot or an old bucket and, tucked out of sight, will provide wildlife benefit even in shaded gardens.

To make a hoverfly lagoon, simply fill a watertight container with water and organic matter – grass clippings seem to work well – and leave it well alone. Alternatively, if there is an area of the garden that is permanently waterlogged, plant it up as a dedicated lagoon using marginal pond plants and leave some open space for the hoverflies to use. Hoverflies should lay their eggs in the lagoon, which will hatch into tiny larvae (called rat-tailed maggots because of their unprepossessing appearance). Once they have hatched into hoverflies in the summer they can get to work munching on the pesky aphid population in your garden.

Q Why won't bumblebees move in?

YOU REALLY WANT TO HELP THE bumblebees, and have put lots of ground-nesting bumblebee houses around your garden – but the bumblebees aren't using them! Why do they not like the houses, and what can you do to provide shelter and nesting sites for bees in your garden?

Things to get right for bumblebees

Even when a nesting box is in a perfect location, occupancy rates still might be as low as 30 per cent, so be patient! First, make sure the garden has lots of nectar-rich flowers, especially in spring but all through the year. Spring flowers that bumblebees love include pulmonaria, daffodils, primroses and foxgloves.

A bumblebee nesting box is best sited on a sheltered south-facing bank, and covered with something (e.g. a paving slab) that will keep the rain off. The box itself needs to be in shade or partial shade, such as at the base of a hedge, so that the larvae inside don't get too hot, and have the entrance at ground level facing east or south east. Place wooden houses on another slab or block so that they don't absorb groundwater.

Inside, the nesting material needs to be dry (bumblebees don't collect the material themselves, they use previously lined burrows and nests from other creatures), such as dry moss, wood shavings or shredded paper.

Attracting other types of bees

Solitary bees are less fussy when it comes to nesting sites; some nest in the soil while others, such as carpenter bees and the red mason bee, like hollow stems. Make a simple bee hotel by cutting canes to fit in a terracotta pot or wooden box, securing them in the base with clay. Put the hotel on its side (so the canes are horizontal) in a quiet spot – hung on a wall and sheltered from the rain is ideal.

A Queen bumblebees are rather fussy when choosing a nesting site, and will often turn up their noses at proprietary boxes or homemade nesting sites. Providing plenty of food as well as shelter will tempt them to live in your garden, and even if you don't attract bumblebees, there are other types of bee that need help and homes.

Is an old-style rockery wildlife-friendly?

THE ROCKERY PART of your garden seems to be a waste of space; it has a lot of rocks and the plants are all quite small. What can you do to make it more wildlife-friendly, or should you replace it with something else?

Smooth newt
Lissotriton vulgaris

Making the rockery the best it can be for wildlife

Rockeries are often planted with alpine species, many of which flower in early spring when there is little other nectar around for bumblebees and other pollinators. Add as many of these plants as possible (e.g. crocus, pulsatilla), as well as other plants that like free-draining soil, such as sedums and thymes. Aim for plentiful rather than sparse planting.

Dwarf shrubs and trees (e.g. conifers) are also usually a feature of rockeries, and can provide shelter in the dry (because the soil is well-drained) for small mammals and birds as well as insects and spiders.

The rocks themselves, especially if they are of different sizes and have gaps, nooks and crannies between them, will also provide homes for beetles, spiders and insects – and thus also attract birds that will feed on them. A rockery near a pond can also offer shady hiding places for frogs, toads and newts.

Major renovations in any garden need careful consideration, as they will disrupt the garden's ecosystem for a while and a rockery can be a useful habitat for a number of species that might not otherwise visit the garden. If it has plenty of places for hiding between the rocks, insect sunbathing spots and a wide variety of plants, a rockery can be an excellent garden feature for wildlife.

SUNBATHING SPOT

Many insects need a place to rest and warm up, especially on cold or cloudy days, and the sunny stones of a rockery are an ideal place for them to do that.

Should you ever kill insects?

THE GLOBAL INSECT POPULATION is declining at an alarming rate. Insects are the basis of all terrestrial food chains, so should we be letting all insects live for the sake of the planet's biodiversity and wildlife and not kill any garden pests?

This is a difficult question, and the answer depends on many different factors. In the case of domestic gardens, it comes down to a question of balance and personal priorities, but it is a good idea to pause before swatting that fly.

Many scientists are warning that the rapid drop in insect numbers could have a far greater effect on the world than the rise in sea temperatures and other effects of climate change. The decline can be seen in diverse habitats around the world, and is easily shown by the fact that there are far fewer bugs squashed on car windscreens in the summer now than there were 20 years ago. The drop in insect populations is likely due to loss of habitat, use of agricultural pesticides as well as the changing climate, and it is estimated that thousands of insect species will go extinct before they are even discovered. They might not be as attractive as other endangered species such as snow leopards or polar bears, but insects are the foundation of all life on earth and as they decline, so too do their predators.

Is it okay to kill garden pests?

This is a moral dilemma that can only be answered by the individual. On the one hand, if pests are ruining homegrown food crops, it might be better to kill the pests in order to be self-sufficient and reduce the family's carbon footprint. On the other hand, killing greenfly that are making the roses look rubbish is probably not worth it, environmentally. It comes down to a question of priorities, and it is worth asking (before reaching out to squash a vine weevil): is this a reflex action, or should I let it live in order to benefit the wider ecosystem? Increasing tolerance of pest damage – and if we start to view insects as vital and fascinating parts of the garden rather than as pests at all – will benefit insects in a small way, and every small action helps. If an insect pest must be controlled, consider using biological controls rather than indiscriminate chemical sprays.

WHAT WE CAN DO TO HELP INSECT POPULATIONS

Planting insect-friendly gardens – plenty of nectar-rich flowers (not forgetting night-flowering plants for moths), creating a pond and making an open compost heap are all good things to incorporate:

• Attract beneficial insects to the garden to help predate on pests.

• Don't be too tidy in the garden, leave places for insects to shelter.

• Add some bug hotels for insects to use as shelter and nesting sites.

• Buy organic food to support farmers who don't use pesticides or other sprays harmful to insects.

• Reduce our carbon footprint and otherwise be environmentally friendly to reduce our impact on the larger environment.

• Use peat-free composts (home-made, preferably) – irreplaceable peat bogs are valuable insect habitats.

• Campaign for insect habitats on a wider scale – write to local councils asking them to plant (and not mow when safety allows) wildflower verges and roundabouts, and support wildlife charities.

Dandelion
Taraxacum officinale

Why aren't my nest boxes being used?

Tree sparrow
Passer montanus

YOU'VE PUT UP NESTING BOXES in your garden to help the birds, but the birds are not using them. What are you doing wrong?

Birds are using the boxes to build a nest and raise their young – they are not going to use a bird box, however well-intentioned, if they do not feel it is safe for them and their chicks for a few months. There are a number of different reasons the birds might be put off:

Siting

The bird box needs to be sited in the right position. Most small garden birds do not usually nest high in the trees, so make sure the box is at a level roughly 2–4m (6–12 ft) above ground. The box should be placed on an east- or north-facing, or shaded, wall to avoid getting too hot during the day. It should also be placed somewhere sheltered so that it doesn't get too cold or wet in windy weather. Angle it away from the wall slightly to also help prevent rain from entering the box.

The birds will prefer a clear flight path to the box, and also a clear view around the base of the box – not shrubs or climbers in which predators could be lurking. It is likely that birds will not use the box in the first nesting season after it is put in position – they will want to assess it over time, after which the timber will also have lost all smells of people.

Other garden users

Birds may be put off from using a box if they don't feel the garden is safe. If they are too often disturbed by you or children – especially going too near the box – they will not nest in it. Equally they may feel vulnerable to cats, squirrels, rodents or dogs, or even larger birds (make sure the entrance hole is not too large on homemade boxes).

Bird boxes are a great way to provide habitats for native birds, but they do need to be properly sited and maintained to be able to attract birds to use them.

Are your nest boxes the right shape for the bird species you want to attract?

Maintenance issues

A nesting box needs an annual clear out to remove the old nest and make sure it is clean and watertight before the next breeding season. Between the beginning of August and the end of January, remove all debris from the box, and swill it out with boiling water to kill any mites that could affect the health of the birds. It's worth checking it once more at the end of January to ensure it hasn't been taken over by squatters – snails and bumblebees also like to use nesting boxes.

Sometimes birds are happy to feed in your garden but will go their own way for food.

ATTRACTING BIRDS

Are the nesting boxes in the garden suitable for the species of birds that already visit? Different birds prefer different styles of boxes, so check that you have the right ones for the birds in your garden. Ensure also that the box is appropriate – there are a few over-styled options on the market that might look good in the garden but will either never be used by birds or could cause them harm.

A basic wooden box of untreated wood is all they need. Attracting a wide range of birds using a bird feeder (keeping it topped up through the year) will also help to encourage them to investigate and use the nesting boxes available.

Q Who overwinters where?

SOME INSECTS ARE SHORT-LIVED, surviving only a few days in the summertime, but many will survive through the winter and need to find suitable places to shelter and hibernate away from the worst of the weather. What can gardeners do to help provide these winter habitats, and who is going to use them?

◀ Many insect species will utilise a bug hotel, and they are easy and inexpensive to create.

A Many wildlife species, including birds, insects and mammals, can do with a little extra help in the winter. Creating specific homes for these creatures and leaving the garden a little messy over winter can help them survive the coldest months.

grasses to rest and shelter over winter. Holes in brick or stone walls, sheds and piles of pots are also used by insects and spiders. Butterflies and moths will find somewhere quiet and dark such as behind shelves in garages or in the folds of curtains or garden umbrellas. Bumblebees bury themselves in tiny burrows in the ground or under leaf litter, beetles like log piles or go underground.

To help, make a bug hotel to provide extra homes in the garden. Leave the stems of herbaceous perennials standing until late winter. If you disturb insects, move them to a similarly cool and dry place quickly or they might perish.

Hidey holes for minibeasts

Many species, such as ladybirds, solitary bees, queen wasps and lacewings favour small holes such as the cracks in wooden window frames; the dried, hollow stems of herbaceous perennials; or the base of ornamental

Cosy corners for amphibians and reptiles

Frogs, toads, newts and slow worms like warm and sheltered places, such as piles of leaves, compost heaps, log piles or under large stones or in the pond. They can also bury themselves under the surface of compost and soil (including in open bags). They will not be hibernating as such, just resting in a state of torpor and venturing out only on warm days.

Provide winter homes like log piles and leaf litter. Take care moving around likely habitats so they don't come to accidental harm (e.g. when turning the compost heap). If you do disturb one, return it to a similar spot gently.

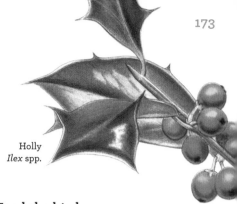

Holly
Ilex spp.

Helpful homes for hedgehogs

Leave piles of leaves and twigs for hedgehogs to hibernate under (always check through a bonfire pile very carefully before lighting it), or provide a hedgehog home or two. Hedgehogs can wake too soon in mild winters and can easily die if they didn't put on enough weight before winter. Putting out food in late summer/autumn helps boost their reserves. If you find a hedgehog in distress or awake in winter contact British Hedgehogs (britishhedgehogs.org.uk) for advice.

Feed the birds

Birds do not hibernate and therefore need plenty of food each day to survive and stay healthy. Help by planting shrubs and trees that bear lots of berries or seeds (e.g. ivy, holly, rowan) and by keeping bird feeders topped up with a range of different foods (seeds, mealworms, fatty blocks, peanut butter and fresh fruit).

OTHER WAYS TO HELP

Melt the ice on ponds (don't crack it – this sends harmful shockwaves) and replace frozen bird bath water every day so creatures have access to fresh water. If you don't have a pond, a saucer on the ground will help creatures living at ground level.

Dormice and bats will find their own homes for hibernation, but will appreciate extra food in autumn to bulk up their reserves.

▶ Pile up logs in a quiet corner of the garden to provide a home for a variety of creatures through the year.

Q What use are ants?

WHAT DO ANTS EAT? Are they just a nuisance or should I be more concerned about their effect on my plants? Do they do any good in the garden, or are they only there to ruin picnics?

Black ant
Lasius niger

A Ants are fascinating, social creatures who work tirelessly for the good of the colony rather than individual gain. They are worth observing and can bring some benefits to the garden – notably localised soil improvement – and are food for birds and other insects, so unless a nest is causing a problem it does not need to be destroyed.

Ant species

The most common ant in the UK is the black ant, which is completely harmless to humans. They do not sting or spray formic acid when on the defensive, they can only bite – and their jaws are too weak to penetrate human skin. Other species include the yellow meadow ant (which builds earth anthills above its underground nests) and the narrow-headed ant, now so rare it is a protected species. The red ant, whose nests are often found under large stones and paving slabs, can give a painful sting.

An invasive alien species of ant, the Asian super ant, has been discovered in the UK, likely imported along with exotic plants. It is super not in size (it's smaller than the black ant) but because its colonies of interconnected nests can stretch for miles, making them likely to outcompete native species. Known nests are being monitored and prevented from spreading; it is likely they will have a negative impact on native ecosystems, so report a nest to your local council if you think you've found one.

▼ There are many species of ants – not all create anthills like this one.

Aphid farmers

In the garden, ants are useful soil engineers, creating tunnels to allow air to be incorporated into the soil, mixing it and adding fertility. They prefer sandy soils and sunny spots to build a nest, with a queen ant underground laying eggs and worker ants going out to find food for themselves and the colony of larvae (they have two stomachs – one for their own digestion and a social stomach in which they carry the food back to the nest). A nest typically contains 4,000–7,000 ants, but can total 15,000 individuals. However, the Asian super ant colonies number in the many tens of thousands.

◀ Ants love sugary fruit, which is why they are often attracted to picnics.

Ants love sugary foods and when they have found a good source they lay a trail for their fellows through chemicals that rub off their bellies as they walk. The excretions of aphids, sugary 'honeydew', is a favourite food, and ants are known to farm aphids, protecting most of them while they harvest their honeydew.

NUPTIAL FLIGHT–FLYING ANT DAY

Once a colony is fully grown (after 2 – 3 years or so), the queen will begin to lay eggs of winged male drones and queens rather than workers. On a humid day sometime during the summer, these drones and new queens will take flight from the nest, mating in mid-air. Somehow the ants manage to co-ordinate their diaries as other nests fly on the same day, mating with each other. New queens then fly off in search of a new nest site, losing their wings and, their only job done, the drones die a day or so afterwards.

◀ Ant colonies are complex social structures ruled by a single queen.

Worker
(female)

Queen

Drone
(male)

Q How can a lawn be wildlife-friendly?

LAWNS CAN SEEM RELATIVELY BARE OF WILDLIFE compared with buzzing borders, and often have most demands made on them from family life in the garden. Can a lawn have any benefit for wildlife, and does that mean not mowing it?

Put away the lawnmower

Insects thrive and breed in long grass, and flowering lawn weeds such as dandelions, daisies and clover also provide them with nectar. In turn, these insects are food for birds. Grasses left long enough to set seed create another food source for birds. Not using the mower also reduces energy use.

There are a few options for allowing a longer lawn:
• Mow the lawn less frequently but at regular intervals using a higher setting that allows some flowers – try over-seeding with white or alsike clover. Do not start mowing until late spring or early summer, creating a meadow for spring.
• Create a summer meadow by mowing once or twice in spring and autumn only.
• Avoid mowing for just a month in spring or summer.
• Get creative and make patterns and paths of mown lawn through the longer sections.

Make a meadow of it

To provide extra flower interest for you and the bees, it helps to add plug plants of wildflowers into the lawn to supplement what is already growing there. Seeding some yellow rattle plants (*Rhinanthus minor*) into the lawn also helps the flowers establish themselves – yellow rattle parasitises on and weakens grass. Alternatively, lift sections of grass and replace them with rolls of wildflower meadow turf.

A

Scruffy, overgrown and weed-filled lawns are the best for wildlife, not perfectly manicured swards, but it is still possible to have a place to play and relax in the garden and create a more wildlife-friendly lawn.

Is a 'dry garden' good for wildlife?

Dry gardens are created in full sun and well-drained or poor soil, using drought-tolerant plants and a gravel mulch. If hot summers and drought are more likely in your area in the future, should you create one for wildlife?

Jerusalem sage
Phlomis fruticosa

Yes, dry gardens can be good for wildlife. Like all habitats, dry gardens will support some species and not others, but for wildlife any garden is better than no garden, and they can be created over old driveways and patios, bringing life to previously barren areas.

Providing food and shelter

There are plenty of plants suitable for dry gardens. Grasses are typical, but incorporate lots of flowers such as erigeron, cotton lavender, phlomis and euphorbias too. Visit examples of dry gardens at RHS Hyde Hall, the Beth Chatto Gardens and Cambridge Botanic Garden for planting inspiration, or look on the RHS website.

Future-proofing

Dry gardens can provide many useful environmental functions. Where they are created in place of paved areas like front gardens or driveways, they can reduce rain run-off, add biodiversity and help to lower urban temperatures. Gravel gardens are also, by the nature of their planting, a relatively drought-proof style of gardening, ready to face the potentially more extreme weather that climate change may put our way.

What wildlife will I help?

Many insects will make a dry garden their home. Under the gravel is a perfect, dry place to hide from the sunlight and view of predators, and on top of the stones they can bask in the warmth. The base of grass clumps and the hollow stems of herbaceous perennials also provide shelter, especially in the winter for ladybirds. Bees, hoverflies and butterflies will visit for the flowers. Spiders will also love this habitat, and predate on the other insects it attracts. Birds will feed on the insects and seedheads.

Woodlouse hunter
Dysdera crocata

Chapter 5

Re-using and Recycling

Q Can I build a pond without plastic?

YOU'D LIKE A WILDLIFE POND in your garden but all the liners
are made from plastic, fibreglass or concrete, none of which are
particularly environmentally friendly. Is it possible to build a pond
using only natural materials and if you do, won't it leak?

A Large ponds can be made
using puddled clay, an age-old
method that needs no plastic.
Small ponds can be made by
recycling existing containers.
If a liner is the only option,
invest in the best affordable
quality to make it last as long
as possible.

Large man-made ponds (and even
canals) that pre-date plastic were
all constructed using puddled clay.
The pond is dug out and a thick layer
of clay spread over the base and sides,
which is then puddled – trodden down
repeatedly until it is solid and contains
no air bubbles.

Puddled clay works best in gardens
already on clay soil (though the
puddling clay will have to be bought
in) and, done properly, should not
leak. However, if the sides are exposed
to the sun they risk drying out and
cracking, creating the potential for
leaks, so make sure it is full and has
plenty of planting around the edges.
You may be able to volunteer with a
local wildlife group, helping to make
one of their ponds and learning the
technique, or follow online tutorials.
Buying and transporting the puddling
clay still carries an environmental and
economic cost.

On sandier soils a liner may be
the only option for a medium to large
pond. If this is the case, invest in a
thick, heavy butyl liner which will
be longer-lasting than the cheaper,
thinner choices and therefore create
less waste in the long run.

Alternatively, use an existing
container to create a pond, such as an
old sink, bucket or farm trough sunk
into the ground. Ensure it is made of a
material that is not going to degrade
and leach chemicals into the water or
soil and that it has steps or a ramp for
creatures to get out of the water.

◀ Sinking the
container into the soil
so it is flush with
ground level will make
it more accessible for
a range of wildlife.

Is it worth buying a shredder?

A GARDEN SHREDDER can quickly chop up garden waste, from autumn leaves to pruned branches and stems and everything in between. This reduces the volume of waste for green bin collections, can save on trips to the local tip and speed up the composting process. However, shredders use fuel or electricity and can be expensive to buy, so are they worth it?

Using a shredder is one way to manage the problem of disposing of bulky, cumbersome branches and cuttings.

Shredders are at their most useful when the garden produces significant quantities of thicker branches and other green waste that won't readily compost. Larger pieces can be chopped up quickly and efficiently before being composted or used as a woodchip mulch or as a surface for a path. Small and medium gardens are unlikely to create sufficient quantities of this kind of garden waste to warrant buying a shredder, as it can be cut up by hand, put in a green bin or taken to the tip for composting by the local council.

There might be one-off or occasional times when a shredder would be useful, such as a garden replanting or rejuvenation, or the annual pruning of fruit trees. Instead of buying one and having to store it for the rest of the year, hiring a machine can be a more economical choice. Alternatively, ask neighbours, friends or the local gardening society if they have a shredder that could be borrowed. A local tool lending scheme or community sharing project might even be able to source one for you.

Domestic garden shredders will only cope with relatively small branches. Consider cutting up larger woody pieces for a log pile or weaving them into a dead hedge, both of which are beneficial for wildlife, or using them as fuel if you have a log burner. Burning woody waste in a bonfire is another option, but only as a last resort.

There's no need for most gardeners to invest in a shredder, and where enough waste is produced to warrant borrowing one, it can be a greener and more economical choice than buying.

Can I have a zero-waste garden?

HAVING A CLEAR-OUT of the garden shed can be a pretty sobering experience if you've decided to try and go plastic-free and reduce your waste. Dozens of plant pots, broken tools, old compost bags: it's the dark side of gardening. Is it even possible to go 'zero waste'?

Being a conscious consumer

Perhaps the worst waste from gardening is what we generate as consumers. By buying lots and lots of plants you create the demand for lots and lots of plastic pots. Grow as much as you can from seeds and cuttings. Buy 'bare-root' plants in autumn and winter, they will have been lifted straight from the field, bypassing the need for plastic pots and compost, so it's a double win.

Avoid really cheap gardening equipment at all costs. That 99p trowel will be in landfill before it's planted its twentieth plant. The cheapest plastic plant pots are so flimsy they'll barely get a courgette seedling through the month or so it needs before being planted out. You're better off using toilet rolls as a much more eco-friendly alternative. Consumer pressure is a useful tool – if your local garden centre doesn't sell bare-root plants or sell compost in reusable 'bags for life' ask them if they will.

Generations of gardeners before us had zero-waste plots. We can too. Conscious consumerism, a willingness to share and some careful thought about what we do and why can all lead you down a zero-waste path – a path that's not only good gardening, it nourishes the soul too.

Zero-waste gardening tends to mean you save money by using what you already have.

◁ Bare-root plants make a cost-effective choice that's also environmentally friendly.

GROW TOGETHER

Swap plants and seeds. It's life-affirming. Seeing someone smile as they receive something you've grown, and the knowledge that you're getting something back in return is a wonderful feeling. And it's made all the sweeter by knowing you're doing something good for our planet. Sharing bigger tools such as shredders and hedge trimmers using tool libraries or sharing schemes is a big win for bank balances *and* the environment. There's no point everyone on your street having a shredder they only use twice a year.

A deeper shade of green

Permaculture gardening (see pp. 88–9) offers many insights into zero-waste gardening. By learning to see your garden as a system in itself, and then part of a bigger system, you can find zero-waste strategies for every part of gardening and living in general. Seek out courses online or in local community gardens.

Waste not

Municipal garden waste composting schemes are pretty green, and the compost they provide back to gardeners is usually cheap and free of weed seeds, which is a big bonus. But if you don't have access to this means of disposal, there are lots of alternatives. Having a compost heap (or two, or three!) is a great way to dispose of most garden waste (see pp. 102–3). If you find yourself with too much kitchen waste and not enough woody material to make good compost, consider a bokashi bin or wormery (see p. 126): both of which make superb, fertile compost, saving yet more waste.

▲ A wormery is a great investment in gardens that are too small for a compost heap.

How can I manage without plastic sacks?

PLASTIC SACKS ARE STILL the only way to buy compost on a small scale, and are also useful to carry and remove waste in the garden when pruning and weeding, so how can they be eliminated from gardening?

There is no escaping the fact that plastic sacks are bad for the environment, but with some forward planning and research into local alternatives, there are ways to avoid using them both for buying compost and for disposing of waste.

Without doubt plastic sacks are a convenient, quick and easy solution and that doing without them takes more forward planning and potentially more effort and monetary outlay. However, they are often not recyclable, not very durable, and so quickly end up in landfill. They are also a petro-chemical derivative.

Re-use your existing sacks as many times as possible, for example, they can be used for making leaf mould, with a few holes punched in the base and side. Turn the bags inside out

🔻 To avoid having to use plastic sacks at all, its worth investing in a metal-based wheelbarrow. Not only will you be saving the planet, but you will also save yourself from any back injuries from heavy lifting.

before filling them, so that the black side is outermost – this will absorb heat more readily and speed up the decomposition of the leaves.

Other options for moving garden waste and compost

Thinking ahead before embarking on some gardening can help reduce the need for shoving all the waste in a sack (and taking it to the tip). Perhaps the garden itself could be changed to reduce the amount of waste for which the sacks are currently used? Or perhaps just a change in methods is necessary – use a trug and/or

wheelbarrow and spade to move things around, which can often be easier on the back and arms than lugging sacks anyway. Lay planks on the grass/soil to avoid making tracks or compacting it unduly if the ground is still a bit damp.

If sacks are still the best option, use heavyweight builders' bags instead – they are still plastic, but more durable and can last many years of use. It's possible to darn them with string and they can also be recycled at the end of their life (unlike most thin plastic compost bags). Re-use your own or ask local builders or builders merchants if they have any they no longer need.

BUYING COMPOST

Of course, the greenest way to source compost for the garden is to have a homemade supply, and there are many compact and fast composting systems available that make this possible for many gardens. When compost must be bought, consider if it would be worth buying in bulk (perhaps shared with a neighbour) when it can be delivered in one-ton bags or even as a loose load, reducing or eliminating the need for packaging completely. Some

garden centres are now beginning to supply loose compost and refillable bags (a bit like taking a re-usable cup to get a takeaway coffee from a café), and hopefully others will follow suit – apply some friendly consumer pressure to your local garden centre and ask about whether they will be running a similar scheme. As an alternative to using growbags for tomatoes, invest in some pots that can be re-used every year and fill them with compost bought as above.

Will a homemade water butt work?

WATER BUTTS AREN'T JUST A MEANS of reducing water bills from summer watering, they also reduce national energy needs (the water has to be processed and pumped before it comes out of the tap), plus rainwater is better for plants and ponds than tap water. Is it possible to make rather than buy a water butt, and do they have to be plastic?

▲ Rainwater is better for the garden than tap water, which contains chemicals such as chlorine that can inhibit plants' ability to absorb nutrients.

With good reason, unfortunately plastic is still the primary material for water butts: it is lightweight to transport, relatively durable, easy to clean and watertight. However, there are proprietary water butts that are made using recycled plastic, and you might want to consider other options, such as re-using wooden barrels and galvanised metal tanks.

A water butt can be as simple as an open-topped container in which rainwater is collected, either by putting it under a downpipe, so it collects the water running off the house, greenhouse or shed, or just leaving it in the open. However, without a lid it is more prone to infestation by midges, getting clogged up with falling leaves, and can also be dangerous for children, pets and wildlife. A better option is to construct something with a lid, into which a circular hole is cut to allow a

There are various options for creating a homemade water butt, either repurposing old drums and canisters, and they tend to be a lot more attractive in the garden than purpose-made ones.

diverted section of the drainpipe to be put through (so that when the butt is full, the overflow continues to the drain). If it is so deep the base can't be reached with a watering can, or the lid is too unwieldy to remove for regular access, the water butt will need a tap at the base to access the water.

REPURPOSED WATER BUTTS

Options for containers that can be repurposed into water butts include oak barrels, metal drums and plastic food containers (often in the form of large blue barrels), which can be sourced from local businesses or online. They will need to be thoroughly cleaned before use, disinfected if necessary, to avoid the water becoming a breeding site for any pathogens; it is best to avoid containers that previously housed oils or chemicals.

Water butt tap kits can be bought from garden centres, and will need to be sealed into their place with a fungicide-free aquatic sealant –

remember to raise the water butt on a stand of bricks or similar so that the watering can fits easily underneath the tap. There is a bit of DIY involved, but there are plenty of online tutorials, or ask a handy friend or neighbour to help.

Be aware that wooden barrels may leak initially. This is because as the wood has dried it has shrunk and needs to swell up again to make it watertight. Just keep topping up the water until it stops leaking from the joins. If the water level in the barrel drops too low it could dry out again, so site the water butt out of direct sunlight and top up if necessary.

◀ Water butts can be made from recycled barrels or old plastic food containers.

Q Does my garden need watering?

SEASONAL WEATHER is becoming increasingly extreme, with long periods of no rain and very hot weather conditions likely to become more common in the future. How often should you water your garden?

A Gardens need a lot less water than you'd think, even during hot, dry spells. Checking the soil and compost to see if a plant actually needs watering is crucial to avoid wasteful watering.

Consecutive days of hot and dry weather may not necessarily mean that garden plants are thirsty. At first they will use up the water in the soil around them and then, with the soil acting as a wick, draw up water from deeper underground. Over-watering can lead to lush foliage, which in turn can mean fewer flowers and a greater risk of pest and disease damage.

What needs watering?

A long period of drought can mean even a mature garden needs some watering, but in general, established plants should need little extra watering through the summer. However, certain plants will need regular attention with the watering can:

• Seedlings and young plants need the soil around them to be kept moist as they haven't yet grown the root systems to draw up lots of water. If the soil around recently-sown seeds dries out they may not germinate properly.

• Newly bedded-in plants that only have access to the water in their plug or small ball of roots and compost until they can spread their roots into the surrounding soil.

▼ Moist soil is vital during the early stages of seedling growth.

▶ The compost in hanging baskets and pots will dry out quickly in hot weather, so they will need watering more often than plants in the ground.

• Plants in pots, hanging baskets and window boxes may need daily or twice-daily watering in hot, dry and/or windy weather.

• Annual vegetables and fruit trees and bushes need regular watering to produce a good harvest.

What about my lawn?

Lawns are often the first part of the garden to look bad in dry weather, but even when brown the grass can quickly recover after some rain; it will only die in a prolonged period of drought. As tempting as it is to put the sprinkler on and keep the lawn lush and green, this is a real strain on water resources and should be avoided. During a hosepipe ban, concentrate on watering the plants, and water the grass only if it has been recently laid or sown (avoid this situation by only establishing new lawns in spring or autumn). Set your mower at a higher setting or don't mow at all. Finally, consider seeding the lawn with herbs and wildflowers

instead of grass to create a mini-meadow – they have lots more benefits to wildlife and are lovely to look at.

Smart watering

Always check the soil/compost at the plants' roots first. Water in the morning or evening once the sun is off the garden to minimise evaporation. Always direct the water at the soil/roots, not the foliage. A layer of mulch every spring can help the soil retain good moisture levels.

DID YOU KNOW?

Plants that droop in the midday heat may not need watering at all, they are simply deliberately wilting in the sun to minimise their surface area and therefore the water lost from their leaves.

Can I make wildlife houses from scrap wood?

YOU DON'T HAVE A WOOD BURNER, and don't want to burn dead wood and prunings from the garden or offcuts from DIY jobs – are they any good for making homes for wildlife?

Log piles

Standing dead wood – a tree that has died but not fallen down – is ideal because it also provides nesting places for birds and bats, but if it's not safe to leave the tree standing, piling up the logs in a quiet corner of the garden is a second option that also really helps wildlife. As the wood rots, it provides food for beetles and other invertebrates, which in turn are food for birds.

Simply stack the logs in a pile in dappled shade – too sunny and the wood will dry out, too shady and it might be too cold for insects. Half burying the bottom tier will help keep the moisture in the pile. Then leave nature to take its course.

Common pipistrelle
Pipistrellus pipistrellus

Yes, scrap wood and other materials can be repurposed and made into a wildlife house. It's actually a great way to use up leftover bits and bobs that would otherwise be waste, just make sure it's safe to use. Dead wood is invaluable for wildlife and leaving some in the garden is also a great idea.

Dead hedges

A dead hedge is old garden prunings, such as woody branches or old herbaceous perennial stems, woven between upright stakes. More garden waste can be pushed down on top as it gradually rots. They are used in forestry work as barriers, but can just as easily be created in a large or medium garden, and will provide shelter and habitat for birds and small mammals.

BIRD, INSECT AND HEDGEHOG BOXES

Untreated wood – which has not been stained, painted or pressure-treated – is best for making wildlife homes. The RSPB has guides for making bird boxes (rspb.org.uk), and you can also stack up old pallets spaced by bricks and layered with twigs, broken pots, canes and more to make a home for insects (a bug hotel) – the Wildlife Trust (wildlifetrusts.org) has plenty of advice.

Hedgehog populations are struggling as many of their natural habitats are lost. A simple fix is to cut a hole in the bottom of boundary fences to allow them to ramble through – encourage your neighbours to do the same –

and provide them with some dry shelter and a place to nest or hibernate.

Use offcuts to build a box, with narrow slits or small holes for air vents in the sides and an entrance hole measuring 15cm (6 in) square, ideally you should also add a 30cm (12 in) long tunnel – like an igloo. Put some dry leaves inside and site it at the base of a hedge or shrub with the entrance facing south if possible. Alternatively, repurpose an old wine crate. The top can be covered with a piece of plastic sheeting (cut open an old bag-for-life) and then a layer of leaves to waterproof it and make it look more natural. (If you have dogs that are likely to attack a hedgehog, it would be best to give the house to a neighbour instead, cats should be less of a risk.)

European hedgehog
Erinaceus europaeus

How long do seeds last?

SOMETIMES YOU CAN GET CARRIED AWAY with the seed catalogue and order more than you can grow that year. If a packet of seeds is past its sow-by date, does it mean the seeds inside are useless or can they still be sown with good results? How can you tell if seeds are going to germinate?

It depends on the seed type, but most will last long after the 'sow by' date on the packet if they have been correctly stored. Do a viability test to see if they will germinate successfully.

All seed packets from large seed companies now have to carry information on them about when the seed was packed and also a 'sow by' date. Even when stored correctly, the viability of seeds will deteriorate over time so ideally, seeds will be sown the same year they are purchased. They will be fresh and have the best chance of germinating into healthy plants, as well as not clogging up the potting bench. Whether or not the seeds inside old or 'out-of-date' packets are viable depends on a number of factors.

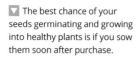 The best chance of your seeds germinating and growing into healthy plants is if you sow them soon after purchase.

The germination process

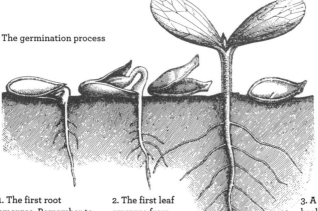

1. The first root emerges. Remember to keep moist until the root system is established.

2. The first leaf emerges from its casing along with its stem.

3. A seedling with healthy leaf, stem and root system begins to grow.

As seeds can often look quite similar, ensure you label each packet as you fill it, and also write the date for future reference.

VIABILITY TESTING

Rather than sowing a whole batch of suspect seeds, sprinkle a few on a piece of damp kitchen towel, folding it over. Put it somewhere dark and warm, keeping the towel damp, for a week or so, then check for signs of life – if the seeds have sprouted, the rest should also germinate successfully when sown.

Storing seeds

Ideally seeds should be kept in their packets or envelopes (labelled for home-saved seed!) in an airtight tin or box. Add a packet of desiccant gel (save them from other purchases) to each tin if possible. Keep the tin in a cold, dry place – around 5°C is ideal – such as a shed, porch or the fridge, until needed.

Seeds that don't keep well

Some seeds, hellebores for example, need sowing straight away, or need to be kept moist. Alpine species tend to have a shorter shelf life than other ornamentals, and among vegetable seeds, onions, leeks and parsnips won't last well.

What's the best way to get rid of garden items I don't want?

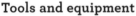

YOU TRY TO RE-USE THINGS IN YOUR GARDEN as much as you can, but sometimes things just have to go. Prunings, old leaves, broken tools and equipment, old pots, excess plants – gardens can create a lot of unwanted stuff. How can you dispose of it in the best way for the environment?

Tools and equipment

Before throwing away and buying a new tool, can it be mended? Online tutorials may be able to help if you're unsure about DIY, or try a local mending shop. These are popping up in various communities, offering expertise and experience for free – just take in your broken item and ask for advice on how to fix it.

Good-quality tools and other equipment in full working order can be sold on auction websites. Working or broken tools can be offered on local trading websites or try to seek out a local community gardening club or gardening/wildlife charity that might appreciate the donation – often someone will be happy to put a new handle on a spade or fix a lawnmower if they're getting it for free. Alternatively, find your nearest 'Tools Shed' collection point on their website. This charity collects old and broken garden hand tools from around the country, fixes them in prison workshops while teaching the inmates

There is likely to be someone out there who wants it! A little internet research or asking around will find them, or there are lots of ways to recycle old items. It takes a little more effort, but it's worth it to avoid things pointlessly filling up landfill.

metal- and woodworking skills, then donates the finished tools to local schools and gardening charities.

Excess plants

Sown too many seeds, or don't want those plants in the border any more but can't bear to compost them? Again, freecycle is a good place to pass on unwanted plants, or sell them with an honesty box at the garden gate. Take them to a seed or plant swap and trade them for plants you do want. A local community gardening scheme

⬛ Spare plants can be donated to local community garden projects.

(either guerrilla or above-board) would probably welcome any spare plants, as would a local gardening club, allotment society or charity sale. Alternatively, volunteer to plant them for an elderly neighbour to brighten up their garden.

When passing on plants, always be sure that they are disease and weed free as far as possible (see also p. 25).

Recycling garden waste

For tools, old pots, garden waste and other things broken beyond repair, always try to recycle before throwing it away. Council household recycling centres can recycle a surprising number of different items, it just might take a little while to sort and separate the different materials. If in any doubt, check on recyclenow.com or just ask the attendants.

PLASTIC POTS

Despite industry moves to replace the un-recyclable plastic pots with more environmentally friendly alternatives, most gardeners have a hoard of black plastic pots lurking somewhere in the garden. Re-use them as much as possible, including to house divided plants you might be passing on. If you still have surplus, some gardening centres will collect them and take them for recycling or donate them to local gardening charities or schools (or you could bypass the garden centre and offer them direct to the charities). Plastic plant pots that are not black can be put in with household recycling. Supporting garden centres and plant nurseries that are trying to do away with plastic by selling plants wrapped in newspaper is also an excellent way to remove the pots from the system altogether.

How can chickens help?

HAVING A FEW HENS clucking contentedly in a corner of the garden – and fresh eggs for breakfast – is many people's idea of the eco-friendly gardening heaven. Does the reality match the ideal, and is keeping chickens actually that environmentally friendly?

Keeping chickens is a good way to cut down food miles and turn slugs, bugs and weeds into healthy, tasty eggs. Just be aware that you need to invest quite a bit of time and effort into getting your setup to be fully fox-proof, otherwise you won't be the only ones enjoying having chickens around.

Chickens are ravenous beasts. This can be a blessing and a curse. They just love to help you dispose of all kinds of garden undesirables such as slugs and snails, as well as many weeds. Let them loose in the garden though, and they'll just as happily tuck into your veg and flowers.

One way to get the best of both worlds is to have a smallish permanent (and fox-proof) run, and some temporary fencing to allow your birds a bit of supervised and controlled time out during the day while you're in the garden or allotment. Fence off small

🔺 Chickens aren't difficult to care for but you must be able to give them daily attention.

areas at a time – your hens will love to help clear beds ready for planting. They'll scratch up the soil, uprooting or eating all the weeds and gobbling up any slugs and snails they find as they go. Their droppings will also add fertility to the soil.

Even when cooped up in their run, any weeds or bugs chickens can get to will be viewed as a treat. When you're weeding the garden, tip your weeds into the run – your girls will love sorting through them to find edible leaves or tasty insects. Leave pieces of wood or empty grapefruit skins placed face down in the garden overnight. Slugs and snails will congregate under them – turn them over and present them to your chickens the following morning as a ready-made platter of delights. Having these supplementary food sources (as well as the lack of food miles) should mean that eggs from your own chickens will have a lower environmental impact than shop bought ones.

SHOULD I FEED MY BIRDS LEFTOVER FOOD WASTE?

Feeding leftover kitchen scraps to chickens has been a tradition for thousands of years, helping to turn food waste into both nutritious eggs and useful fertiliser. However it is currently illegal to do this in the UK unless your household is vegan. This might seem harsh, but with more diseases than ever currently circulating the globe it seems wise to only feed your chickens 100 per cent plant-based waste. If you want to get rid of kitchen scraps containing meat or dairy, bokashi composting bins offer an eco-friendly means of disposal.

▶ Chickens love to roam; they'll eat bugs and weeds but be careful to keep them off prized plants.

I want raised beds – which are the best materials?

RAISED BEDS ARE A GOOD OPTION for accessibility, raising the soil level where the ground is poor or badly drained, adding in growing spaces to paved areas and for growing plants in a different soil type from that of the rest of the garden. Should they always be made from wood, or are other materials an option? Can recycled wood be used, and if so are there any caveats?

Buying new raised beds

There are many proprietary kits for constructing raised beds in standard shapes, and also firms that can supply the materials to build bespoke shapes and designs, or new wood can be used for DIY beds. When choosing one of these, research their environmental credentials. Is the wood they use sustainably sourced and certified by the Forestry Stewardship Council (FSC)? What chemicals and methods do they use to treat the wood, if at all? Are they accredited by any other bodies, such as the Soil Association?

Treated wood can contain chemicals that, once the wood is wet, will leach into the soil, potentially harming soil organisms and making

Raised beds can be made from various materials, including wood, brick, stone and recycled plastic kits. All have environmental costs and benefits, so it is a question of weighing up the pros and cons particular to your garden and making the most conscious choice possible.

Raised beds can be used to grow almost anything, such as this culinary herb garden.

their way into any food crops grown in the beds. Pressure treating pushes the chemicals deep into the wood from where they are less likely to leach, but the safest option is to use untreated hardwood. It may be more expensive but it will degrade much more slowly than softwood (such as pine) and there are no concerns with unnatural substances.

Building wooden beds from recycled wood

For DIY raised beds you also have the option of using recycled wood. Traditional choices include old railway sleepers, although due to high demand and low supply it is more likely that sleepers bought today are actually new timber cut to shape. Sleepers are a poor choice in many respects – they are so thick they take up a lot of space that could be actual bed and growing space, they are unwieldy and tend to dictate the shape of the bed, and true old sleepers were treated with toxic tar and creosote that will leach.

Other options for recycled wood include old scaffolding boards – these are easier to use but, as for new wood, ask what they have been treated with and if it can't be established err on the side of caution. Scrap, salvage or reclamation yards are a good place to start, as are community swapping and trading websites. The beds could be made using treated wood and then lined to provide some form of barrier between the wood and the soil, but as that lining will inevitably be plastic, it has its own environmental cost.

OTHER OPTIONS

Some companies supply raised bed kits made from recycled plastic, or the beds could be built from brick, stone or paving slabs on edge. The latter three options have the advantage of being long-lasting with no leaching risk, but they do require foundations – if concrete is used this has a significant environmental cost to consider.

How realistic is self-sufficiency in a medium-sized garden?

YOU ARE REALLY INSPIRED BY TV PROGRAMMES such as *The Good Life* and *River Cottage*, seeing people living off the land and growing their own food, but your garden isn't large. Would it be possible to grow enough food to live off all year round, and is it a good idea to try?

It depends on how big your family is, but in theory it is possible to be self-sufficient in fruit and vegetables with a plot of 250m² (300 yards²). You are not going to have enough space for livestock or to grow cereal crops for milling into flour, but growing a large portion of your own fruit and veg will definitely reduce your environmental impact.

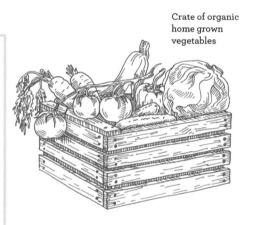

Crate of organic home grown vegetables

It is easy to see the attraction of growing your own fruit and vegetables, and harvesting seasonal (organic if you like) food in the fresh air a few paces from the back door rather than picking up packaged food in a fluorescent-lit supermarket that might have been flown half way across the world. Home-grown food reduces our reliance on supermarkets, we are no longer at the mercy of global food price changes, and we know the exact provenance of our fruit and veg. It is hard work though, and the plot will need plenty of attention throughout the year.

Does size matter?

A traditional allotment is 250m² (300 yards²) – roughly as big as a doubles tennis court – with this size being determined as adequate to feed a family of four with vegetables and soft fruit, although research in the 1970s estimated the total area needed for one person to eat (vegetarian) all year round, including space for paths and storage, was 720m² (850 yards²).

It's what you do with it that counts!

There are many ways to take steps towards self-sufficiency, and by planting to maximise the space, it is possible to get some really heavy harvests from even a small area. For example, if you have no space for an orchard, grow fruit trees as step-overs for bed edging, or train them against walls and fences instead. Consider adopting a forest-garden planting scheme, using three tiers of productive perennial plants in one area of the garden. Careful planning, successional sowing and catch cropping can all make the best use of space in annual vegetable beds. Extending the season with early-, mid- and late- varieties of the same crop and also by growing under protection such as a greenhouse or polytunnel helps to spread the harvests and avoid gluts. If

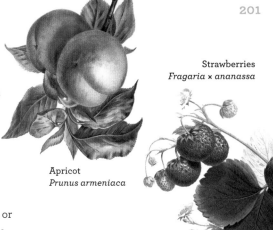

Strawberries
Fragaria × ananassa

Apricot
Prunus armeniaca

▲ To use up a glut of fruit, the most obvious and rewarding thing you can do is make your own jam.

you are aiming for true self-sufficiency, you will need to dedicate a substantial part of the plot for growing so-called calorie crops (e.g. potatoes). Use reference books to help you plan your sowing and growing and to maximise your yields.

IS IT WORTH IT?

It is certainly enormously satisfying to grow one's own food, and it definitely reduces a family's environmental impact. Growing food is a brilliant way to get children interested in gardening and connected with the natural world. It can connect us with the seasons and teach new skills, such as making jam and pickle.

It can also reduce food bills in the long run, but that depends on the initial outlay on infrastructure and perennial plants/trees.

Aiming to grow a good proportion of the family's food for most of the year is probably more achievable – and enjoyable – than enforcing a strict rule of self-sufficiency.

Are there alternatives to plastic?

YOU ARE SERIOUSLY WORRIED about all the plastic waste in the world, and particularly the oceans. How can you reduce your use of plastic in your garden – are there plastic-free options?

It is estimated there are around 500 million plastic pots currently in the world, which will take more than 400 years to break down. Pots are not the only plastic in the garden though, there are plastic compost bags (see p. 92), trays, watering cans, cane toppers, fertiliser tubs and bottles, plant and seed labels and more. Plastic is cheap, waterproof and lightweight – it is easy to see why it is so pervasive – and the alternatives are generally more expensive, as well as having their own environmental costs in terms of transport weight and manufacturing energy. However, non-plastic alternatives are a good investment, often lasting a lifetime, and by sourcing products from local, sustainably minded companies some of those costs can be mitigated.

Yes, plenty, with more coming on the market all the time. However, don't throw something away (by recycling it) just because it's plastic – use it until the end of its life and then replace it with a non-plastic alternative. RHS writer Sally Nex has started the website gardeningwithoutplastic.com, which is a fantastic source of information.

▶ Toilet roll tubes are actually better than plastic seed trays for deep-rooted seedlings such as sweet peas and sweetcorn.

PLASTIC-FREE ALTERNATIVES

Plant packaging Buy bare-root plants, divide plants or propagate existing garden plants (either your own or your friends'!). Use online plant companies and nurseries that commit to sending out plants in plastic-free packaging.

Seed sowing Use wooden seed trays (homemade or bought), and/or make individual seedling pots out of old newspaper using a paper potter. Or, save up the inner tubes of loo roll, which are especially good for long root plants such as sweet peas and sweetcorn.

Pots Terracotta pots are the longest-lasting, but can be a hefty investment. Coir pots have a relatively large environmental footprint; for a like-for-like swap of plastic to biodegradable pots try Vipots, which are made from plant waste. Otherwise, homemade pots from cardboard (such as cereal boxes or corrugated card) will last long enough to grow on a seedling or cutting.

Plant labels Plain lollipop sticks or proprietary options made from wood or bamboo will all biodegrade once they have finished their usefulness – write

▶ Eggshells and cartons can be used for raising seedlings or microgreens.

on them in pencil to re-use them. Slate labels are more expensive but attractive.

Plant supports Use natural twine to tie in plants rather than plastic; it will only need replacing after a year or two. Buy jute pea netting; weave your own supports for border plants from willow or birch (find a local weaving workshop to learn how), or buy metal supports.

Plant protection Fleece and plastic cloches are not recyclable and short-lived, so invest in glass cloches or a greenhouse, and don't bed out tender plants too soon. Use newspaper, straw and hessian to wrap up tender plants over winter.

Watering and other garden care Buy metal watering cans and non-plastic water butts (see p. 186), and stop using the hose altogether – hand watering is good exercise and actually more effective and accurate. Buy powdered/granular organic fertiliser in cardboard boxes.

Can I make discarded decking into a woodpile?

DECKING WAS ESPECIALLY FASHIONABLE in the 1990s and 2000s as a relatively cheap and cheerful way to easily create different levels in the garden and add dining and play areas in a different way from the crazy-paving patios of previous decades. If and when it gets ripped out or replaced, what are the options for disposing of the boards? Can they be made into a wildlife feature?

WPC decking boards cannot be recycled

Unfortunately all the materials used for decking are made from are unsuitable for making into log piles for wildlife and need to be disposed of elsewhere. It depends what your decking is made from as to whether or not it can be recycled.

Types of decking boards

Decking boards may not actually be made from wood at all, although they resemble it. Timber decking could be hardwood or softwood, both of which would have at least been treated with preservation chemicals before they were installed, and possibly painted with stains afterwards. Other boards may be made from a wood-plastic composite (WPC), or be made entirely from PVC plastic.

Life after decking

Treated woods are unfortunately no good for creating a wood pile for wildlife – the chemical preservatives are designed to prevent the wood from rotting, the very thing that invertebrates, fungi and other organisms need the wood to do in order to thrive. This wood will need to be disposed of elsewhere, such as the timber skip at the local household recycling centre. Wood Polymer Composite (WPC) boards are also not wildlife friendly due to their plastic content, but also unfortunately cannot be recycled due to the way the wood and plastic are mixed together. PVC plastic boards are no good for a log pile, but can be recycled.

Before taking a trip to the tip, consider if there is another use that some or all of the decking could be put to, such as making a potting bench, shed shelves or a cold frame.

Why are bees in the bird box?

YOU'VE PUT BOXES FOR BIRDS AND INSECTS around your garden, but you've noticed that the bees are using the bird box instead of the bee box. What is happening and why?

First, are you certain that it is bees using the box? Wasps make their nests from tiny wood scrapings mixed with their saliva, and gather the wood from all manner of garden furniture and wooden structures, including bird boxes.

If it is bees, they are likely to be tree bumblebees, as honeybees would view a bird box as too small for a potential hive. This species, unlike most bumblebees, which nest in the ground, makes its nest in trees but also takes advantage of other dry, woody spots like the eaves or lofts of houses... and bird boxes. The queen bee will have chosen it for the same reason a bird would have done – it's dry and warm, with a small, easily guarded entrance hole – but because tree bumblebees start looking for nest sites from early March, they can often beat the birds to it. Bumblebee nests are actually quite an uncommon thing to find, so enjoy the fact you have one in your garden. The bees will be gone in four to five months. It is best to keep your distance in order to keep the bees calm – if they are on edge due to frequent activity nearby they could become more aggressive, but if left alone they will not pose any threat. Bees coming in

Unfortunately, despite our best efforts to help, nature won't always do what it is told, and some species will often repurpose wildlife structures of their own accord. Using natural materials for bug hotels can help encourage insects to use them, but sometimes it's best to just enjoy wildlife's ingenuity.

and out of the nest are unlikely to do so in great volume unless they are about to leave. If the nest absolutely must be moved, contact the local Bee Keepers Association for help in the first instance.

Bumblebees, nest box lodgers

What makes the best natural plant supports?

YOU'D LIKE TO USE NATURAL PLANT SUPPORTS, but are not sure how to go about it. Which types of wood are best, and how do you make a support?

Plant supports fall into three main categories: obelisks for climbers such as French beans and clematis; cage-type constructions to hold up taller herbaceous perennials in the border such as peonies; and rows of sticks to support plants like peas in the vegetable garden. Then there are stakes – sturdier pieces of wood to which the single stems of sunflowers or young trees are tied. All of these supports can easily be made from wood sourced from trees or shrubs, either from your own garden or using locally gathered material and ultimately, all the material will safely biodegrade.

When a sturdy single stake is needed a simple piece of untreated wood can be used with the plant tied loosely to it. As the plant grows, more ties can be added.

Sourcing as much of the garden's own needs from the garden itself is a great way to make it more sustainable, and reduce costs.

Grow your own stakes

Making space in the garden for a hazel, willow, silver birch or chestnut can provide a lifetime's supply of pea sticks and beanpoles: a traditional coppice. Three or more plants will allow for a full harvest every year on a rotation system, or cut only some of the stems from the plant each year. Cut back to as close to the base as possible to remove the stems, new ones will grow up in their place for future supplies.

Making a cage support for herbaceous perennials

This type of support uses twiggy branches longer than pea sticks but not as long or thick as the stems needed to make an obelisk. Always put in supports before the plant needs it, as then it will grow through or round the support rather than needing tying in. In early spring, as the plant comes into growth, cut a handful of twiggy stems. Their length depends on the ultimate height of the perennial – aim to have

REDUCE THE NEED FOR SUPPORTS

By changing the way plants are grown and managed it is possible to reduce the need for supports or even eliminate them altogether:

• Train climbers up walls, fences or trees instead of obelisks (and try growing climbing beans up sweetcorn plants).

• Don't use too much nitrogen fertiliser or overwater, as it encourages lush, floppy growth.

• Employ the Chelsea Chop technique, cutting back a third of the new growth of late-flowering perennials in mid-May (traditionally the week of the Chelsea Flower Show), to reduce their final height.

the top of the support around halfway up the plant. Push the stems into the ground in a circle around the plant with 20–30cm (8–12 in) between each one. Then bend over the tops of two opposite stems and twist them around each other to hold them in place over the plant. Repeat with the other stems, weaving them in among each other to hold it all together: get creative! The plant will grow up and through the support, rendering it invisible by midsummer, and the cage can be removed and replaced (the stems will be brittle and not last a second year) in late winter.

▽ The young growth of willow is easily bent and twisted to make obelisks and other natural plant supports.

Does recycling have to involve old tyres?

I KNOW LOTS OF THINGS can be repurposed and put to use in the garden, but I'm not keen on the look of large tyres as planters. What other options are there?

Repurposing or upcycling items that would otherwise be thrown away or recycled can be a thrifty way to create planting space in a garden, but it takes careful curating to avoid it looking like a neglected space.

▼ Short-lived crops such as salad leaves and annual herbs can be grown in tin cans and sturdy trays.

Seeing the potential – what can be used?

Aesthetically, it's often a good idea to use more than one of the same item in groups of odd numbers, so save up things you want to repurpose until you have enough. As long as it's thoroughly cleaned and safe to use in the garden (for example it hasn't previously contained chemicals or oils, and isn't made of something that will leach into the soil), there are few limits for an upcycled garden. Finally, ensure potential planters have adequate drainage, by drilling holes in the base if necessary. Choose and use items only when they fit with an overall scheme to avoid them jarring on the eye, and don't plant up recycled items for the sake of recycling them, especially if they are not going to adequately support that plant in the long- or even short-term. Old wellies are a classic example of this, as they are easily over- or under-watered, and they topple over.

Kitchen garden

For food crops, it's nice to use related planters such as large food tins (try local deli and restaurants for olive tins etc.), or wooden wine boxes for baby salad leaf production – while you're at it, corks make great cane toppers.

Cottage garden chic

To stay in keeping with a cottage garden, use natural materials, weathered or in a soft colour palette. An old garden fork can be stuck in the border and used as a plant support, or a tin bath made into a miniature pond or planter. Old wood and glass doors and windows can be fixed together on a frame to create a small greenhouse, then painted in one colour to give it an harmonious look. Broken pots can be turned into a miniature rockery landscape for alpine plants or succulents; an old bookshelf can be painted and turned into an auricula theatre or display for small pots of seasonal flowers.

Homes for houseplants

Lined with a waterproof membrane, old pieces of furniture can be planted up with succulents and cacti: a chest of drawers perhaps, or the upholstered seat cavity of an old dining chair.

A garden for the children

This is where old tyres can be a good idea – they are soft, low to the ground and have a rim for a seat and to enable reaching to the middle – all ideal for a child-friendly flower bed. They can also be disguised – plant them with trailing nasturtiums (on the side facing the house), or paint them in toning colours, or bright ones. Alternatively, plant them into mini-lawns with grass or chamomile, several around the patio, for green seats.

▶ Old tyres are ideal for a child's garden, where they can be planted as mini-lawns or used to grow flowers and vegetables.

Can I use my plants as natural dyes?

BLACKBERRY JUICE STAINS your children's clothes when you're out foraging and you've heard you can use onion skins to dye fabric. What other plants can you use from your garden to dye things, and how do you go about it?

All sort of plants, including trees, perennials, vegetables and even moss yield dyes, but for it to work properly the right plants need to be used. The same plant can yield dyes of different colours and the shade and intensity can vary widely depending on how it was grown and when it was harvested, so it's best to view natural dyeing as an experiment rather than aiming for a particular colour. Most plants create a dye in a shade of yellow or orange. Here are a few to try:

Yellows/oranges: marigolds (*Calendula* spp.), dandelion, yarrow, turmeric, brown onion skins, *Eucalyptus cinerara.*

Reds: madder.

Pinks and purples: purple coneflower, hibiscus, beetroot, elderberries, red cabbage (head), blackberry leaves.

Greens: cabbage leaves, sunflowers, carrot tops, goldenrod.

Blues: purple carrots.

Historically, plants were the only source of dyes for skin, hair and fabrics, such as blue war paint or intricate henna tattoos. Modern synthetics have largely replaced plants for commercial fabric dyeing, but using garden plants to dye fabrics is a fun and interesting craft, a sustainable approach to fashion, and creates fabrics with a unique character.

Purple coneflower
Echinacea purpurea

Yarrow
Achillea millefolium

◀ Natural materials such as cotton yarn can be dyed in a range of earthy colours using vegetable scraps and plants from the garden.

HOW TO DO IT

The best way to get started is to watch an online tutorial, or to sign up for a natural dyeing course. Various public gardens in the UK have areas dedicated to dye plants, such as the Chelsea Physic Garden and Oxford Botanic Garden.

The dyeing process can be as simple as adding the fabric to a pot with the plant dye and some water, and simmering it all together over a low heat for a while. For a permanent dye, the dye and fabric need to be prepared separately before combining.

• To make the dye, chop up the plant into small pieces, add twice the volume of water and bring to the boil. Reduce the heat and simmer for at least one hour, stirring occasionally. Strain out the plant and return the dye to the pan. (Use a stainless steel pan – not your ceramic cookery pots! – and a separate wooden spoon.)

• Use any white or cream natural material: cotton, linen or wool. To keep the dye in the fabric, it needs to be prepared with a fixative (mordant). Berry dyes need the fabric to be prepared in a solution of one part salt to sixteen parts water; vegetable and leaf dyes use one part vinegar to four parts water. Simply simmer the fabric in the fixative mixture for an hour, then rinse in cold water.

• Put the rinsed, fixed fabric into the dye pan, and bring back to a simmer, leaving it until it reaches the desired colour. Leave it to soak, off the heat, overnight for a stronger colour – it will be lighter when it's dry. Wash the fabric by hand, using cold water and a natural detergent, and leave to dry. (Wash it like this in the future too, drying out of direct sunlight, to best preserve the colour.)

Q Can I give plants away?

YOU SOMETIMES HAVE EXTRA SEEDLINGS, **or have
divided a perennial and have some spare sections.
Is it okay to pot these up and give them away? Are
there any plants you shouldn't give to friends and family?**

◀ Home-raised plants make lovely presents for friends and family, but gift responsibly.

Check the government website for an up-to-date list of which invasive and non-native plants to avoid, such as the common rhododendron (*Rhododendron ponticum*), a known host of the *Phytophthora* disease. If in doubt, don't give it away.

When receiving plant gifts, always quarantine them first.

Always buy plants from reputable sources and check them thoroughly first for signs of ill-health (make sure online suppliers have a no-quibble return policy).

Responsible plant gifting (and receiving)

As worldwide trade in plants continues to grow, a number of devastating diseases have caused problems for gardeners and the horticultural industry, such as the disease *Phytophthora* and ash dieback. Invasive pests can also be brought into to a country hidden in plants, from where they quickly spread and multiply, such as the Asian hornet, a predator of honeybees and other insects.

Never give away invasive plants or those that are diseased or infested with a pest – burn diseased material and deal with infestations first.

If a plant is invasive in your garden, tell the recipient, or don't give it away.

A What could be nicer than giving away some spare seedlings, a plant grown from a cutting, or a divided section of a pretty perennial, to a friend or neighbour? Plants make lovely gifts, but sometimes giving plants from one's own garden is not a good idea, and responsible gardeners should follow a few guidelines.

GIVING PLANTS

Advantages of giving plants from the garden

- It's a delightful and low-cost gift.
- It finds a home for surplus plants and saves them from being composted.
- It can help encourage others to take up gardening.
- More plants in the world is a good thing for us and for wildlife.

Disadvantages of giving plants from the garden

- The recipient may not have the experience or knowledge to look after it (help them if they don't!).
- The recipient's garden may not have a suitable place for the plants – it could have the wrong soil type or not enough sun or shade.
- It might not fit with the recipient's planting scheme.

Taking cuttings

Public gardens and plant shops occasionally experience the loss of whole plants, or more commonly see cuttings or seeds being taken surreptitiously from a plant. This is theft. It can also cause irreparable damage to the plants as well as depriving income to small business owners. The plants are often rare and removing or damaging them can deny horticulturists the chance to propagate and expand the stock for the benefit of the world's biodiversity. Don't be tempted to sneak a cutting – either buy the whole plant or talk to the owner/gardener, they may be able to give you a cutting and at least then you know they are happy with you having it.

If the owner/gardener is happy, here's how to take cuttings responsibly:

1. Carefully tear off a side shoot 15cm (6 in) long retaining a small heel of bark from the main stem.

2. Trim the tail end of the heel.

3. Dip into hormone rooting powder and pot up.

Can everything be given a second life?

I'M RENOVATING MY NEW HOUSE and it's creating a lot of waste. Assuming something is safe to use in the garden, how can I repurpose it to avoid taking it to the tip?

▲ Even the most unlikely object can be used as a plant pot – as long as it can hold soil and is fairly watertight.

Furniture and more

Old chests of drawers can be moved out to the shed or greenhouse to make a potting bench and storage for hand tools, spare pots and seeds.

Old doors that have lost their glass can have jute netting attached to the back and fixed to a fence as a frame for a climber. Old ladders are also great for climbers.

Picture frames can be hung to make a feature of a potted plant mounted on a wall – inside or out – and old mirrors can be fixed to a fence or side of the shed. Angle them so they reflect the plants or a vista and they'll bring the illusion of more space to the garden.

An old lamp base with a ceramic platter glued to the top can be turned into a bird bath.

Repurposing the recycling

Old newspapers and cereal boxes can be made into paper and (larger) cardboard pots for seedlings and young plants.

If you've access to a lot of plastic bottles (the larger ones are better, but 500ml bottles will work too), they can

There are lots of ideas for using old furniture and other items in the garden. Browsing sites like Pinterest can be a good source of inspiration, but sometimes the idea comes from the item itself.

be threaded onto canes which are then fixed to a frame to make a greenhouse. The frame could be made with waste batons from a building project, or a mini-greenhouse could even be made using an old wendy-house frame.

IN THE GARAGE

Spare tubing or an old hosepipe can be transformed into a drip irrigation system by adding extra holes along its length. Laid around the plants in a border and covered with mulch, it will feed out water at a steady rate once connected to the tap.

Metal tyre rims can be fixed to the wall next to outdoor taps and used as a hose winder to keep it out of the way and kink-free.

Old tyres can be used as planters (see p. 209) but also can be used to make a raised pathway over ground that gets regularly boggy. Lay a line of tyres on their sides (flat) for the path, with a line each side of the tyres on their edge half buried under the soil to stop the central ones slipping. Fill in the middle and around the flat tyres with soil and seed with grass seed, planting the borders either side, and it will soon look relatively natural.

▼ Scrap wood and plastic bottles can be used to make a vertical herb garden. Explore the many benefits of recycling before you commit to the landfill option.

What's the best way to encourage the next generation?

WHEN IT COMES TO A LOVE and respect for the environment, children are often seen as being a little too screen-obsessed and out of touch with nature. However, we should have more faith in the next generation – how can we help them learn about gardening and supporting wildlife?

Every child is different, and every child can be given the opportunity to come to love the outdoors. Often, all that is required to spark an interest is simply going out together and seeing something amazing, like a butterfly landing on their hand, or a seed they sowed growing into a giant sunflower.

Get outdoors

From a very early age, children can love being outside (playing in the mud!). Spending time in the garden or local nature reserve, just playing or lying on the grass watching the bugs is setting them up for a lifelong love of the environment. More structured activities in the garden, such as seed sowing or creating wildlife habitats (get them helping to build a hedgehog home for example), can spark enthusiasm. Older children might find the entrepreneurial side of growing appealing – selling raw produce or using it to make things with added value like jam or wildflower seed bombs.

Giving children of any age some ownership in the garden (a space to do with what they like) is a good way to let them find their own route without too much pressure.

◀ Ensure young gardeners have decent tools so they don't get frustrated at not being able to do the job properly.

Helping with harvests – especially of things that can be eaten straight from the garden such as peas or fruit, or of the slightly unusual such as cucamelons – is also a good way to entice children into the garden. Show them that failure is okay – sometimes seeds don't germinate or flowers get eaten – and that it is just part of the wider experience of gardening: it's important not to get disheartened and give up.

If they are not keen, find a way to incorporate the outdoors, wildlife or gardening into their existing interests. For example, young bakers might like to know about edible flowers and herbs they could use in their cakes; mathematicians could be encouraged to produce some statistics on garden wildlife through a survey; scientists can do biology experiments to learn about photosynthesis or observe frogspawn and pupating caterpillars; keen readers can be given a copy

Cucamelons
Melothria scabra

of *The Secret Garden* by Frances Hodgson Burnett or other garden- or wildlife-themed literature, or simply encouraged to read outside and enjoy the environment.

Get involved

Gardening and wildlife charities, such as the RHS and local Wildlife Trusts, have regular events for children and also clubs and membership options. If there isn't a gardening club or forest school at school, why not start one? Organisations such as the RSPB run regular surveys in which children can get involved, such as the Big Garden Birdwatch.

CHILDREN IN THE WIDER ENVIRONMENTAL MOVEMENT

Many young people are now passionately involved in environmental campaigning, inspired by teens like the environmental activist Greta Thunberg, and yet may not realise the difference they can make for the wider environment by taking up wildlife or kitchen gardening at home. Teaching young people how to garden and how to grow their own food is an enormous contribution we can make to their future, and shows them small personal actions that will make a positive difference.

Further Reading

*An Ear to the Ground: Garden Science
for Ordinary Mortals*
Ken Thompson
Transworld Publishers, 2003

Bob's Basics: Composting
Bob Flowerdew
Kyle Books, 2010

Butterfly Gardening
Jenny Steel
Brambleby Books, 2016

*Charles Dowding's Vegetable Garden Diary:
No Dig, Healthy Soil, Fewer Weeds (2nd edition)*
Charles Dowding
No Dig Garden, 2017

Companion to Wildlife Gardening
Chris Baines
Frances Lincoln, 2016

Dream Plants for the Natural Garden
Piet Oudolf and Henk Gerritsen
Frances Lincoln, 2013

RHS Encyclopedia of Gardening
Christopher Brickell
Dorling Kindersley, 2012

Gardening for Wildlife
Adrian Thomas
Bloomsbury Publishing, 2017

*RHS Get Growing: A Family Guide to Gardening
Inside and Out*
Holly Farrell
White Lion Publishing, 2020

RHS Grow Your Own Veg and Fruit Bible
Carol Klein
Mitchell Beazley, 2020

RHS Grow Your Own: Crops in Pots
Kay Maguire
Octopus Publishing Group, 2013

RHS How Do Worms Work?
Guy Barter
Mitchell Beazley, 2016

RHS How Can I Help Hedgehogs?
Helen Bostock and Sophie Collins
Mitchell Beazley, 2019

*How to Create an Eco Garden: The Practical
Guide to Greener, Planet-Friendly Gardening*
John Walker
Aquamarine, 2011

The Kew Gardener's Guide to Growing Herbs
Holly Farrell
White Lion Press, 2019

*Life in the Soil: A Guide for Naturalists
and Gardeners*
James B. Nardi
University of Chicago Press, 2007

Making Wildlife Ponds
Jenny Steel
Brambleby Books, 2016

A Natural History of the Hedgerow
John Wright
Profile Books, 2016

*RHS Pests & Diseases: The Definitive Guide
to Prevention and Treatment (2nd edition)*
Pippa Greenwood and Andrew Halstead
Dorling Kindersley, 2018

RHS Plants from Pips
Holly Farrell
Mitchell Beazley, 2015

The Wildlife Gardener
Kate Bradbury
Pen and Sword Books, 2017

Wildlife Gardening for Everyone and Everything
Kate Bradbury
Bloomsbury Publishing, 2019

ABOUT THE AUTHORS

Gareth Richards

Gareth Richards is a qualified
horticulturist, RHS website editor
and freelance writer. A keen
gardener and allotment holder, he
gardened in France, Italy and New
Zealand before settling back in the
UK. His passions include wildlife
gardening and keeping bees and
chickens along with growing fruit
and vegetables.

Holly Farrell

Holly Farrell trained at RHS
Garden Wisley. Her books include
*RHS Get Growing, RHS Gardening
for Mindfulness, The Jam Maker's
Garden, Growing Herbs (Kew
Gardener's Guides)* and *RHS Plants
from Pips*. She also contributes to
magazines such as *The Garden,
The English Garden, Kitchen Garden*
and *Breathe*.

Kate Bradbury

Kate Bradbury is passionate about organic, wildlife-friendly gardening
and is the author of *The Wildlife Gardener*. She writes for a number
of publications including the Guardian and can occasionally be heard
talking about garden wildlife on *Gardeners' Question Time*.

Index

Index

Credits